Pool Perspectives: Vol. 2

Author: Scott Cohen

Graphic Artist: Jose Hernandez

Illustrators: Jana Moungdang and Navin Kistan

Editor: Marie NyBlom

The landscape designs in this book were created by Scott Cohen unless otherwise noted. To see more of our work go to www.GreenSceneLandscape.com or Fetch-A-Sketch.com

PICTURE PERFECT:
HOW TO USE THE PERSPECTIVE DRAWINGS IN THIS BOOK TO INCREASE YOUR SALES

One of the biggest challenges landscape professionals face is in creating presentations that are powerful enough to convince clients to take the next step. The ideas you have for a property might be truly spectacular. But unless your clients can actually visualize themselves in that beautiful new landscape, your plans could be dead in the water.

Fetch-A-Sketch can help. You can use the high quality, perspective drawings available through Fetch-A-Sketch to enhance your portfolio, create winning presentations, and boost sales. Here are some tips for getting started.

WHY SHOULD I USE PERSPECTIVE DRAWINGS?

Sales: The secret of successful sales in pool and landscape design is to effectively communicate the concept to the client. You need the client to dream with you and to see themselves in the landscape you envision for them.

One of the best ways to do this is through perspective drawings. Clients often need a little help to visualize a plan accurately. When you show

Garden artisan Scott Cohen presenting full color perspective drawings from this book on HGTV's *Get-Out, Way-Out!* TV show!

Cohen attributes much of his sales success to the use of perspective drawings. As he says, "To sell them the yard of their dreams, you have to help them dream of themselves in the yard!"

them a flat plan or a top down view, sometimes they simply can't see it. But with perspectives they can really put themselves into the picture. They can see themselves relaxing in their spa or sitting around the fire and truly enjoying a new lifestyle.

Image: High quality drawings can significantly enhance the professional image of your company. Clients appreciate a high-end presentation. It is a sign that you respect their time and will put that same effort into their property. Perspective drawings make it easier to gain project approval from other key stakeholders as well. For example, when homeowners associations are presented with perspective drawings, they tend to accept a project more readily because they have a much better sense of how good it will look.

Excellence: Good drawings are also an important tool for ensuring quality. During construction, perspectives serve as a visual model for everyone involved in the project. Although workers will always need to refer to the working drawings for complete specifications, having perspectives available will give everyone a sense of what your finished product should look like. This helps ensure a consistent concept from design through completion.

Perspective drawings can also reduce expensive changes during the project by giving your client a clear understanding of the outcome they can expect. This helps make the project a positive experience for both client and contractor.

HOW DO I GET STARTED?

Build a portfolio: You can start by choosing a collection of drawings that illustrate the kind of work your company can provide. Browse Fetch-A-Sketch web sites and books to find drawings geared toward the work you want to do in styles that suit your own taste and the taste of the communities you serve. You can then download or photocopy them in a variety of sizes, in either black-and-white or color, to fit your current needs. During your initial sales call, this instant portfolio will give you and the client visual tools to help spark discussion. It will also set a polished, professional for the meeting, ensuring a solid first impression.

Prepare Winning Presentations: While initial sketches and a professional portfolio immediately begin to attract clients, it's during the actual sales presentation that bold, beautiful perspectives will really capture their imagination. Show them the Fetch-A-Sketch drawings and ask, Can you picture yourself here? They need to see themselves vacationing in their backyard and swimming in that pool. They need to feel like they are a part of that drawing.

Even when clients are obviously excited about a plan, it is natural for some to be hesitant about this big decision. Perspective drawings can help give clients a chance to fall in love with their new plan and to develop a sense of ownership of their proposed new landscape. This can be a very powerful motivator.

You may want to let clients take a design home for a day or two to think about it and let it meet the family. This gives everyone a chance to imagine what it will be like to enjoy their new space. We all know what happens when you try to decide on a new puppy by taking it home on a trial basis. This approach has the same effect.

Make sure to explain to your client that the loan is temporary and that the plan is yours, not theirs to sell or give away to another contractor. If you have chosen your designs carefully, the plan will return soon along with an eager client asking, When can we start?

WHAT SIZE DRAWINGS ARE BEST?

This depends on what you are using your images for. For your base portfolio, smaller images are portable and economical. A portfolio can be as simple as two dozen drawings in various sizes that represent pools, spas, barbeques, ponds, and other features you want to highlight. These can be easily carried to initial visits and presented as needed. Images can be rotated in or out depending on the specific interests of each client.

On the set: Homeowners Mary and Arthur Hirsch show off Scott Cohen's full color perspective drawings to HGTV's *Get Out, Way Out!* host Brandon Johnson

To get the most power from your perspectives during the sales presentation, though, bigger is always better. One or two full-size posters professionally mounted on foam board will make a very compelling case. The larger the drawing, the easier it is for clients to fall into the picture. The bigger the project, the bigger the drawings need to be. Large drawings can be supplemented with smaller ones to highlight particular features and round out the presentation. High resolution digital images are available to download online and print in poster size at your local printers.

IS IT BEST TO USE FULL-COLOR?

Color does have a very powerful impact, but there are some cases where black and white can actually be a better choice. During an initial presentation, you may want to use black and white drawings, especially if you are still discovering a client's taste and style. This gives clients a visual frame of reference without committing to a specific color or theme—one that could turn them off. You can then doctor the drawings as you learn more about your clients likes and dislikes.

When you are doing a final presentation and you have a solid sense of what the client likes, nothing is more captivating then color.

WOULDN'T PHOTOS BE MORE EFFECTIVE?

While photos have a place, many designers prefer to emphasize perspective drawings for a variety of reasons. Drawings are meant to be conceptual and they offer more license in how the finished project will look. They give the designer a chance to wow the client now and the freedom to tweak details later. Drawings can also work better for conveying ideas. Sometimes clients can be so distracted by poor photography, bad lighting, and other details that they miss the big picture. Photos show work that has been done before and might have less appeal to clients. Finally, drawings are more personal and simply have more eye appeal for most people. They have the ability to speak to clients emotionally as well as visually.

WILL THE IMAGES FIT THE SPACE I AM DESIGNING FOR?

Again, perspective images are designed to convey concepts, not concrete details. They may convey an attractive fireplace style, an interesting pool shape, or a fun layout for a family play-space. These concepts are generic enough to suit a variety of settings but are specific enough to give clients a clear understanding of the features and style you have in mind for their property. Once the client agrees to an overall design, the contractor can determine the exact specifications to fit the space allowed and match the client's exact style preferences.

HOW CAN I BE SURE OF DESIGN QUALITY?

Because Fetch-A-Sketch only includes drawings that have been pre-screened for quality, users can be sure that the plans they choose are among the best in the industry. Many Fetch-A-Sketch designers have earned regional and national awards for their work and all have earned a reputation for delivering designs with high performance and high style.

GORGEOUS, SKILLFULLY DRAWN PERSPECTIVE IMAGES REPRESENTING THE BEST IN OUTDOOR DESIGN CAN HELP TAKE YOUR COMPANY TO A NEW LEVEL. THEY CAN ALLOW YOU TO CREATE STUNNING OUTDOOR ENVIRONMENTS AND HELP YOU CREATE SUCCESSFUL, BEAUTIFUL, AND WELL-EXECUTED PROJECTS FROM THE INITIAL DESIGN STAGES RIGHT UP THROUGH THE COMPLETED INSTALLATION.

I WISH YOU THE VERY BEST SUCCESS WORKING WITH THE DRAWINGS IN THIS BOOK. CHECK THE BACK OF THIS BOOK FOR A FETCH-A-SKETCH COUPON TO BUY MORE DRAWINGS IN CATEGORIES SUCH AS OUTDOOR KITCHENS, FIREPLACES, PONDS, WATERFALLS AND FRONT YARDS.

CELEBRATE LIFE ALFRESCO!

Scott Cohen

GARDEN ARTISAN,
GREENSCENELANDSCAPE.COM

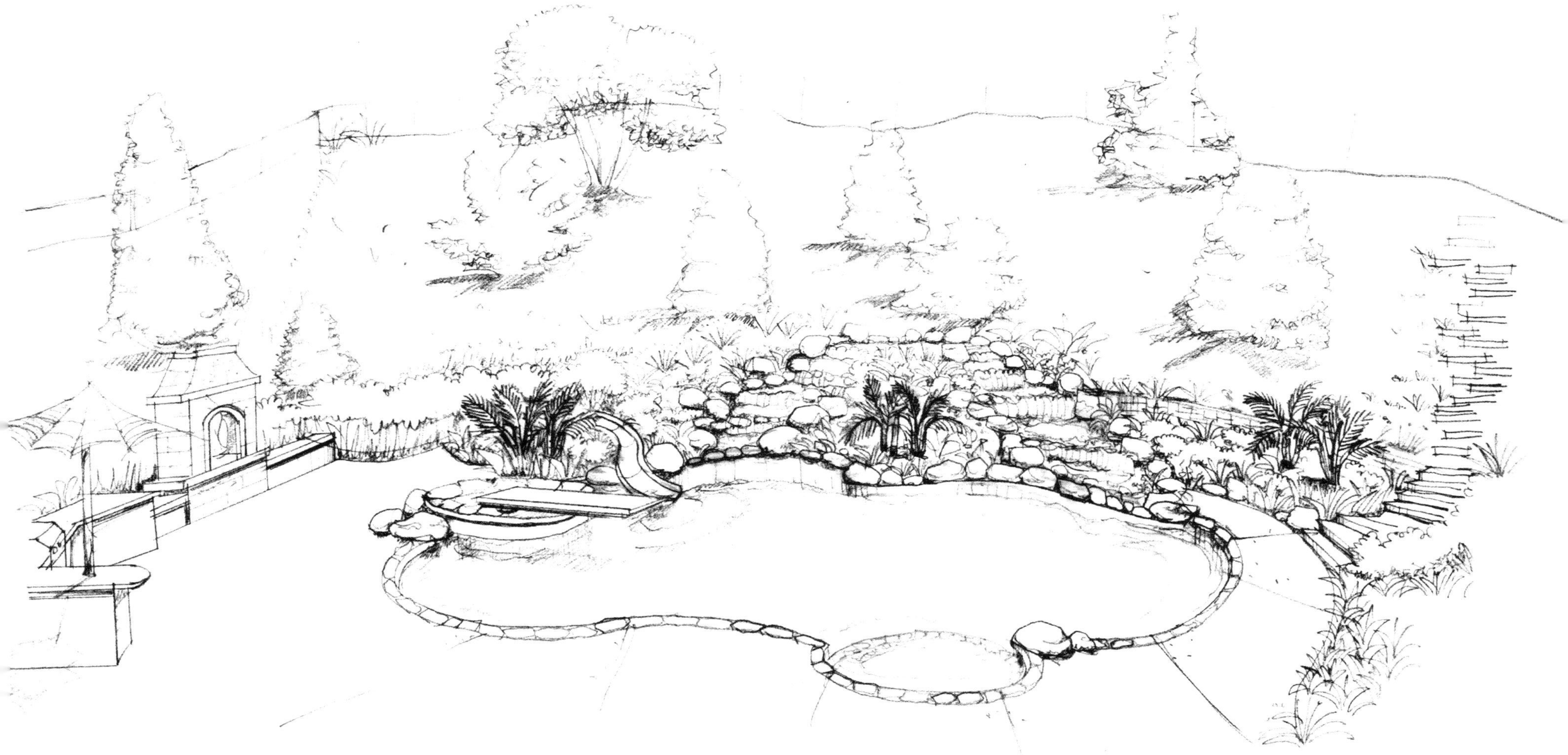

© Fetch-a-Sketch.com

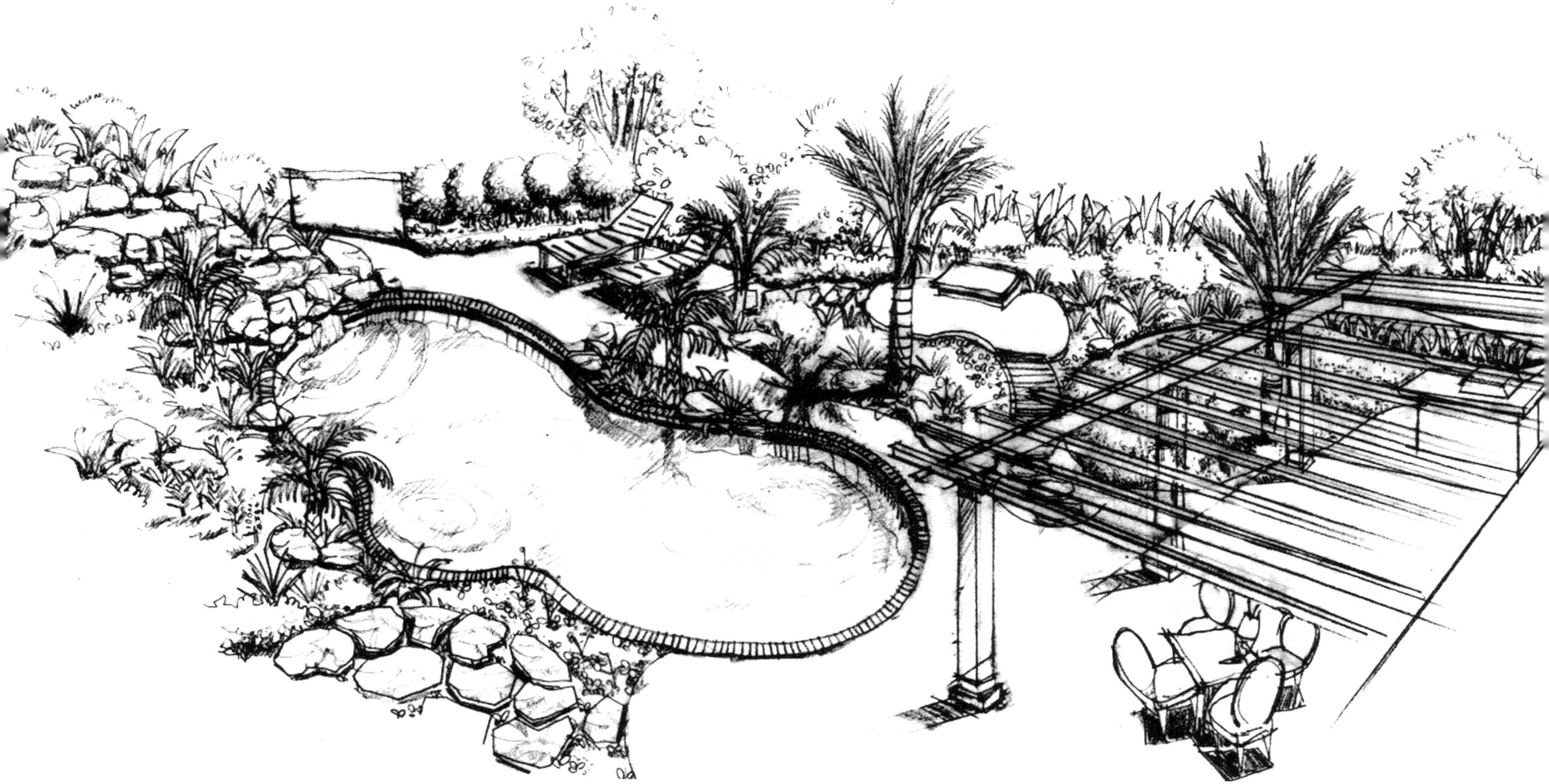

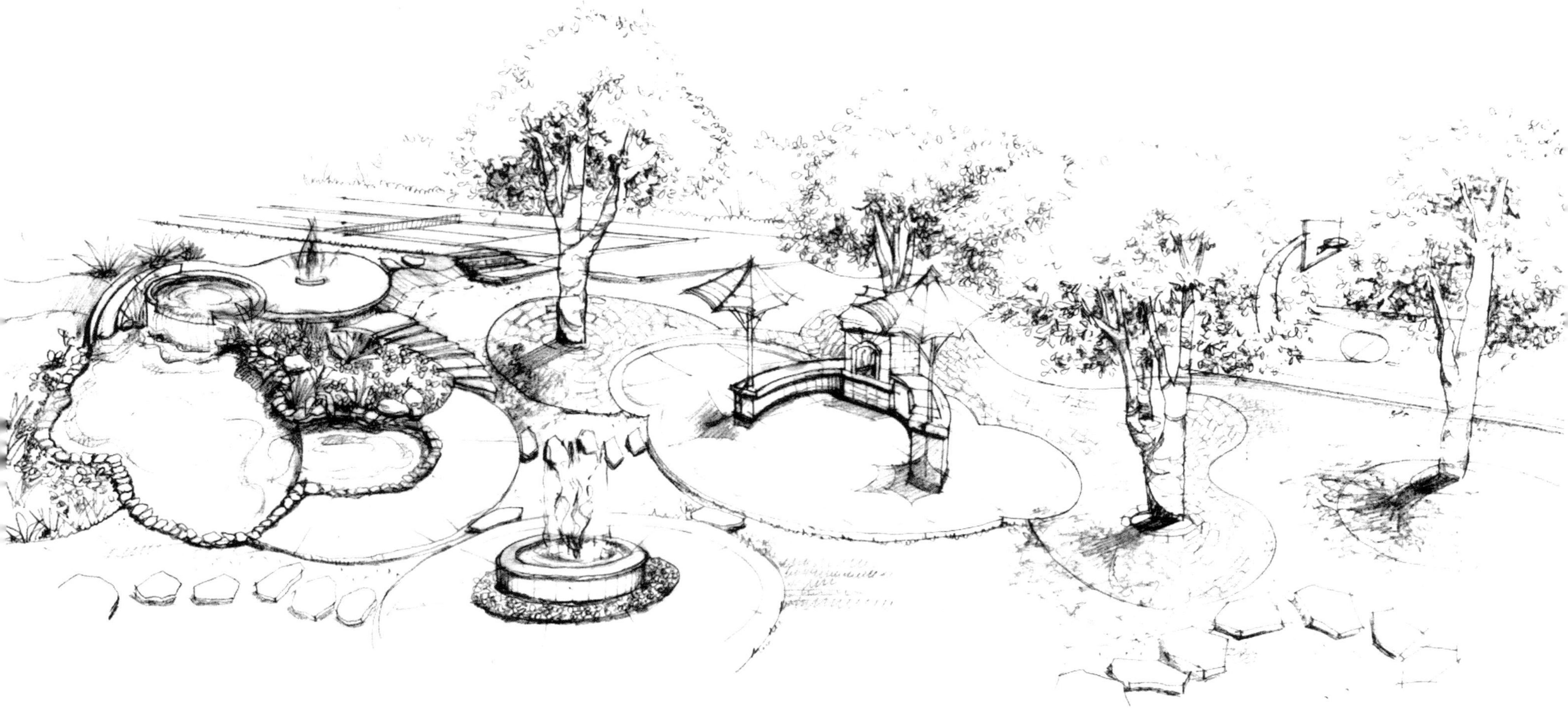

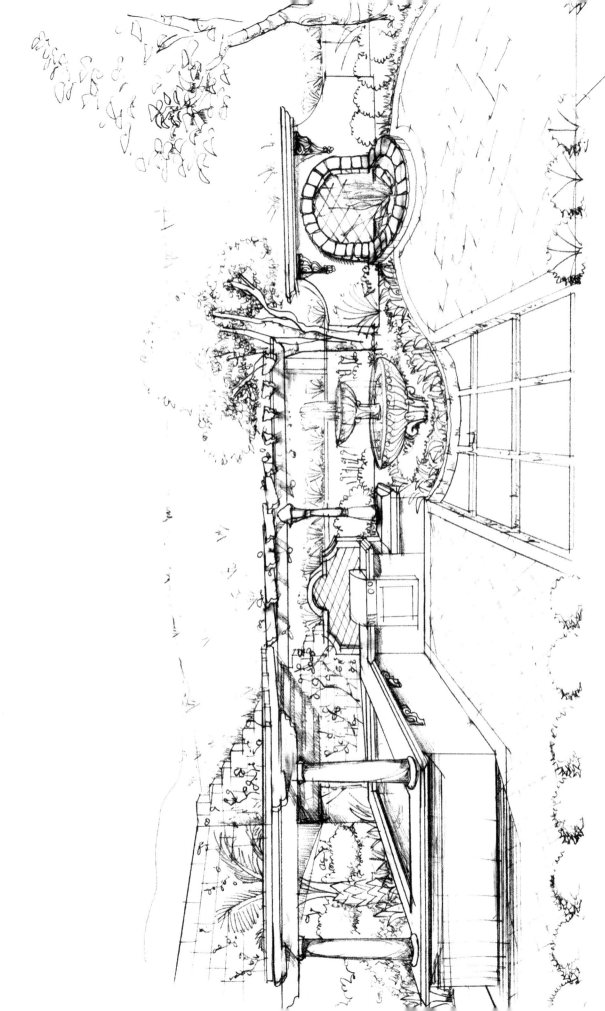

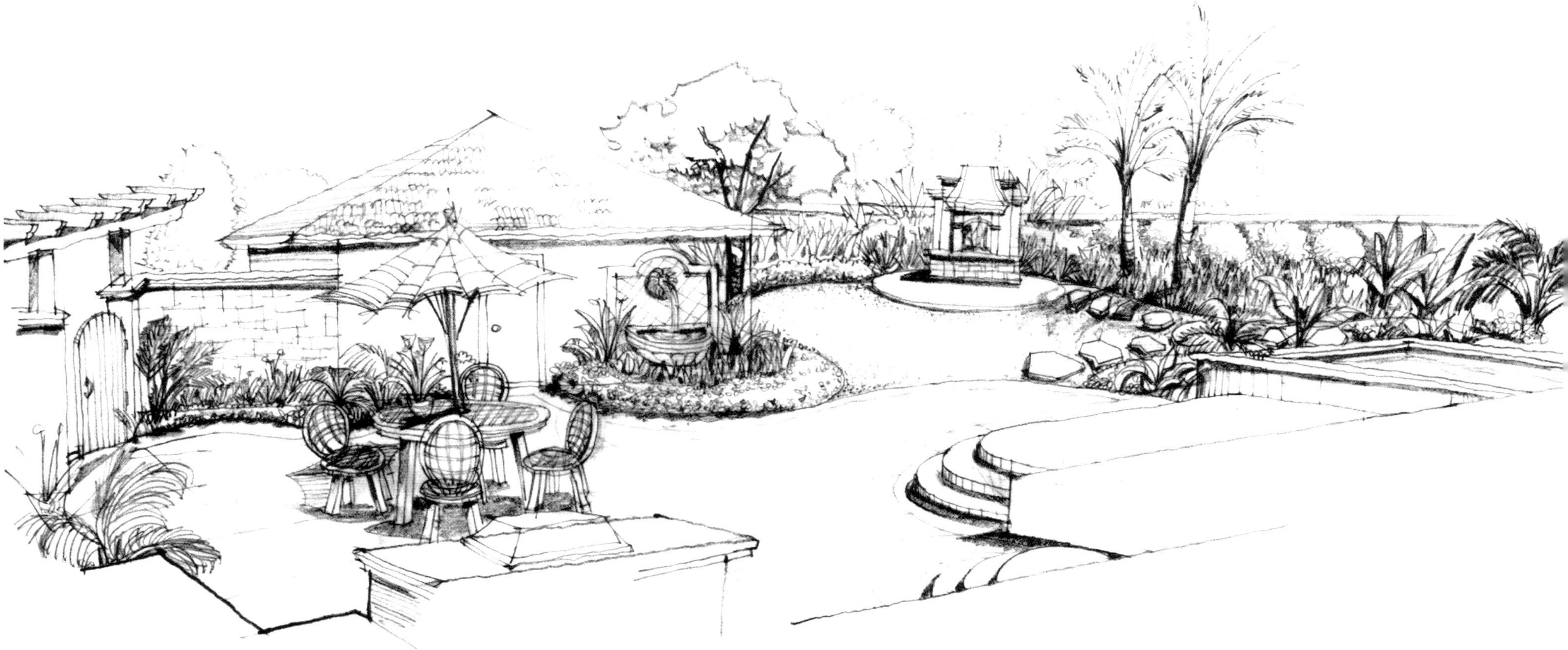

© Fetch-a-Sketch.com

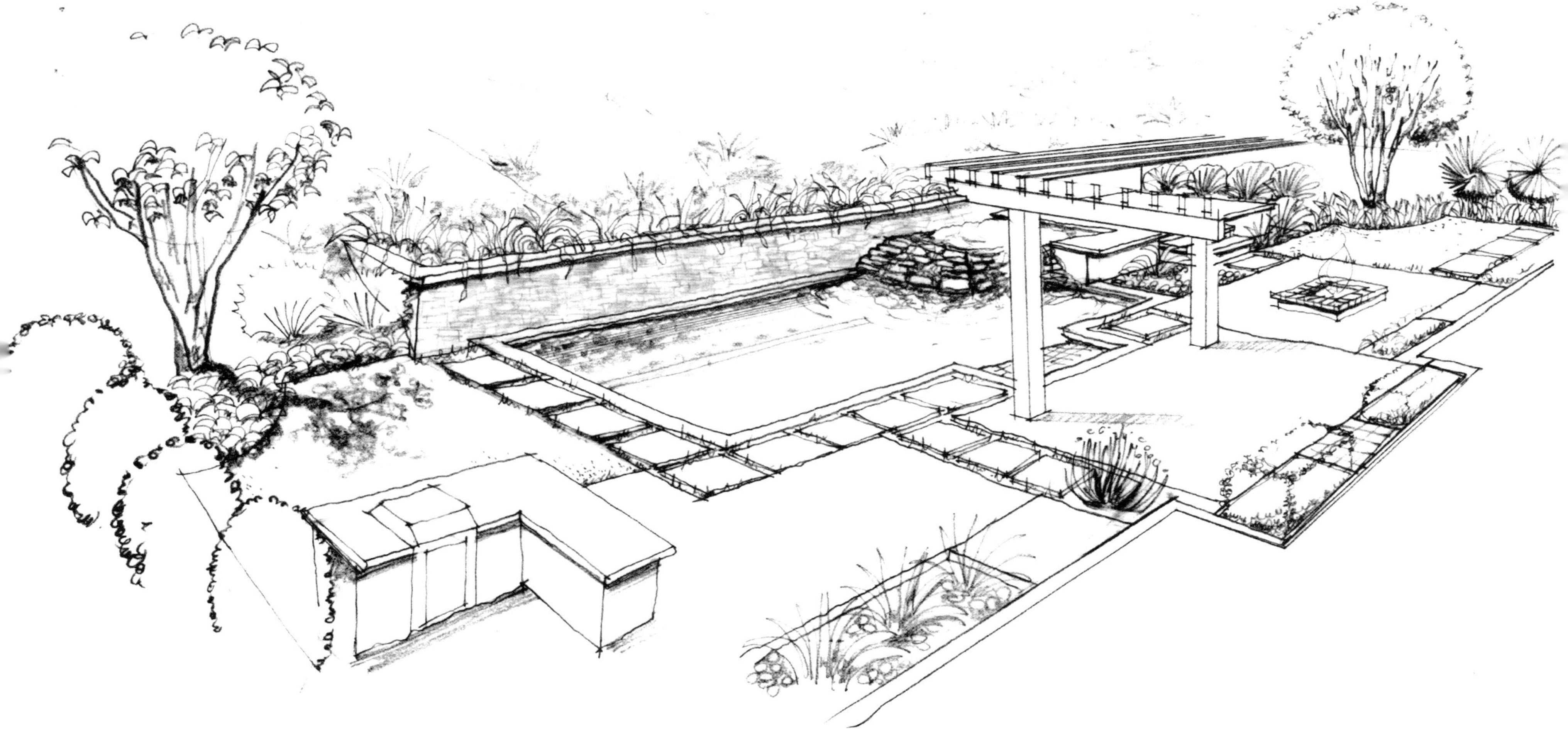

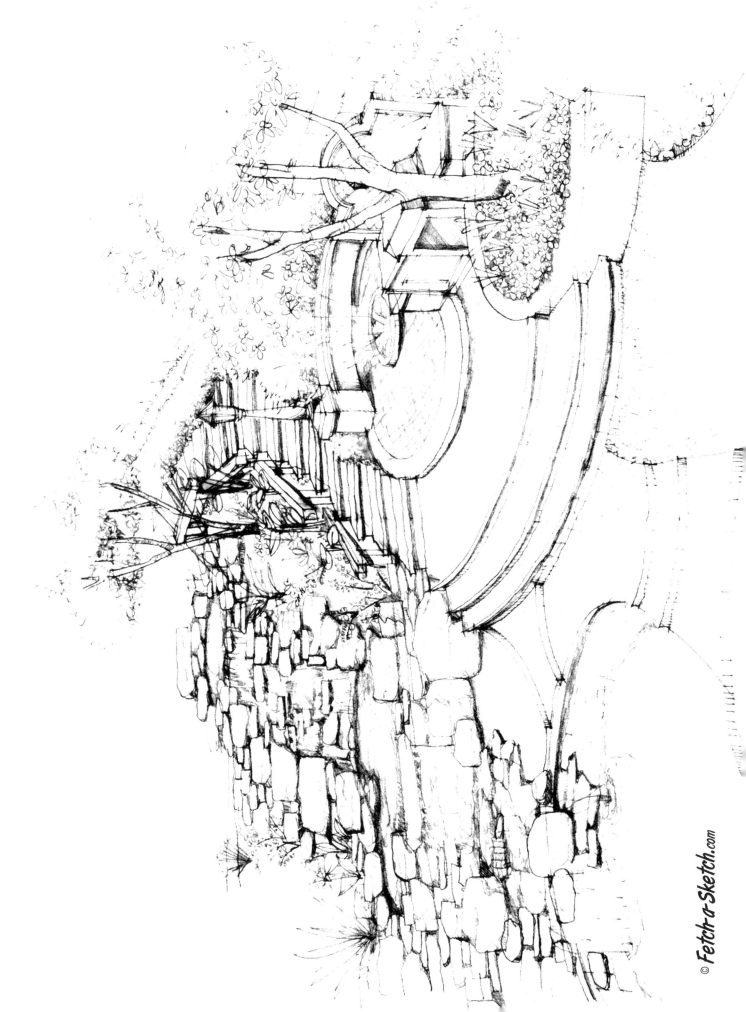

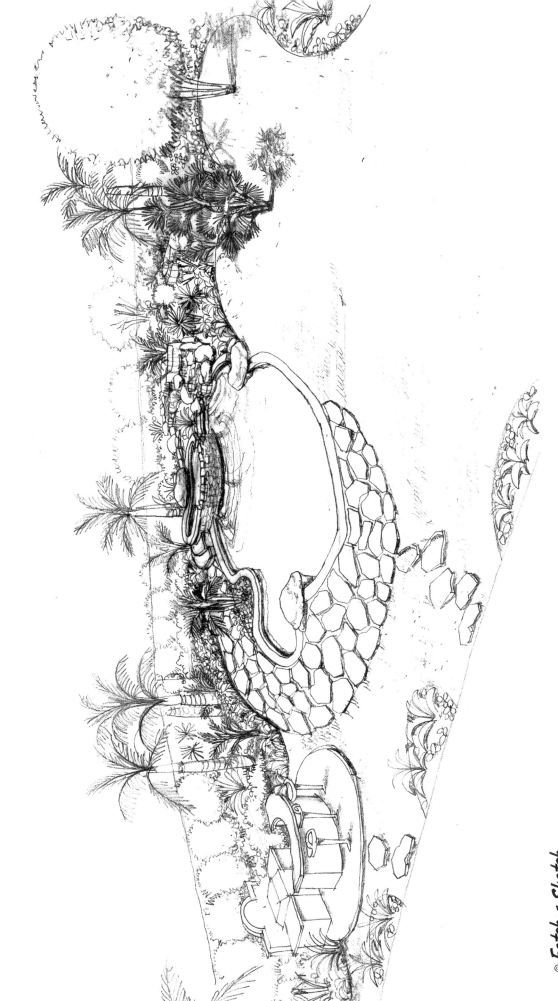

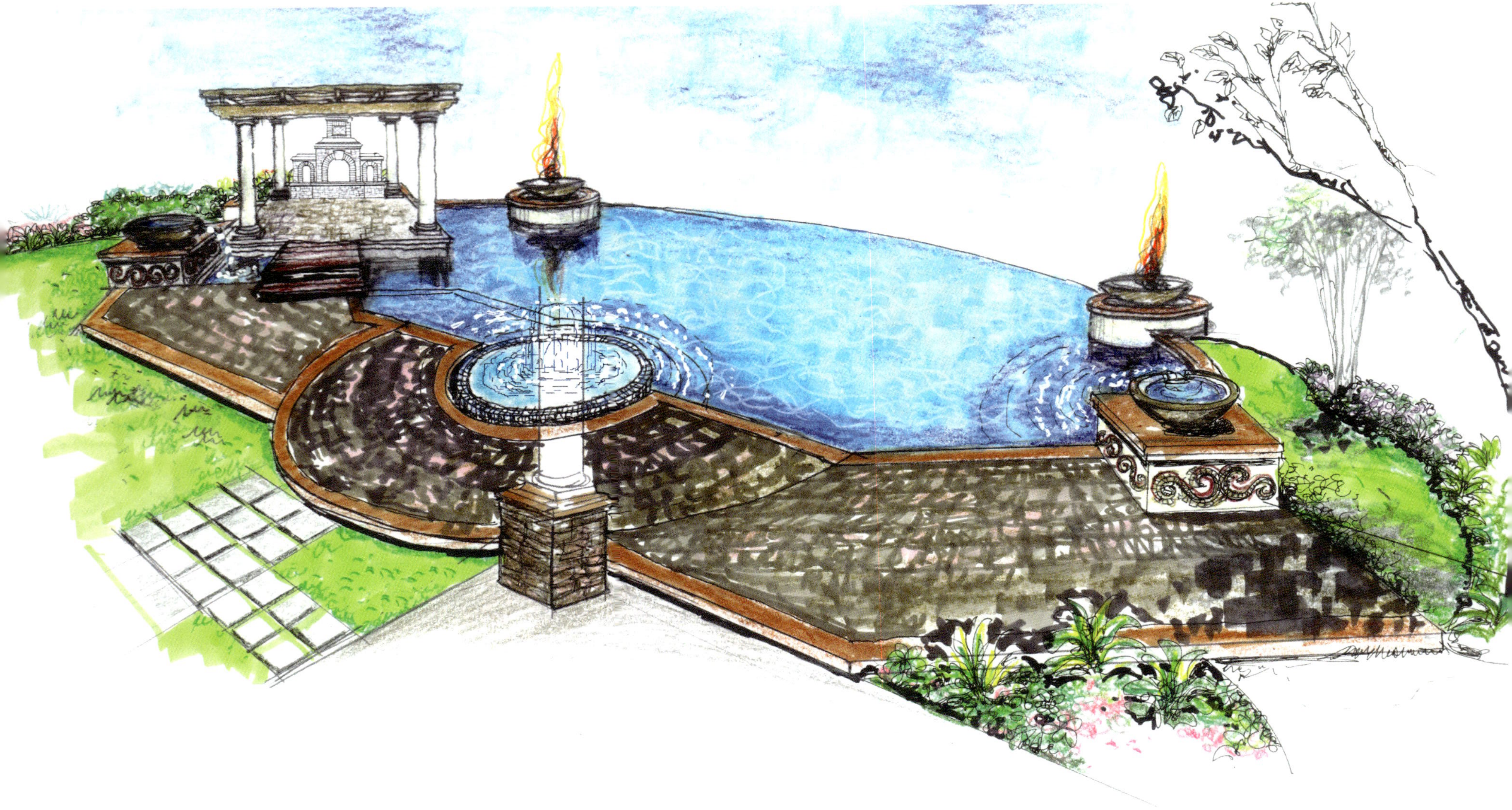

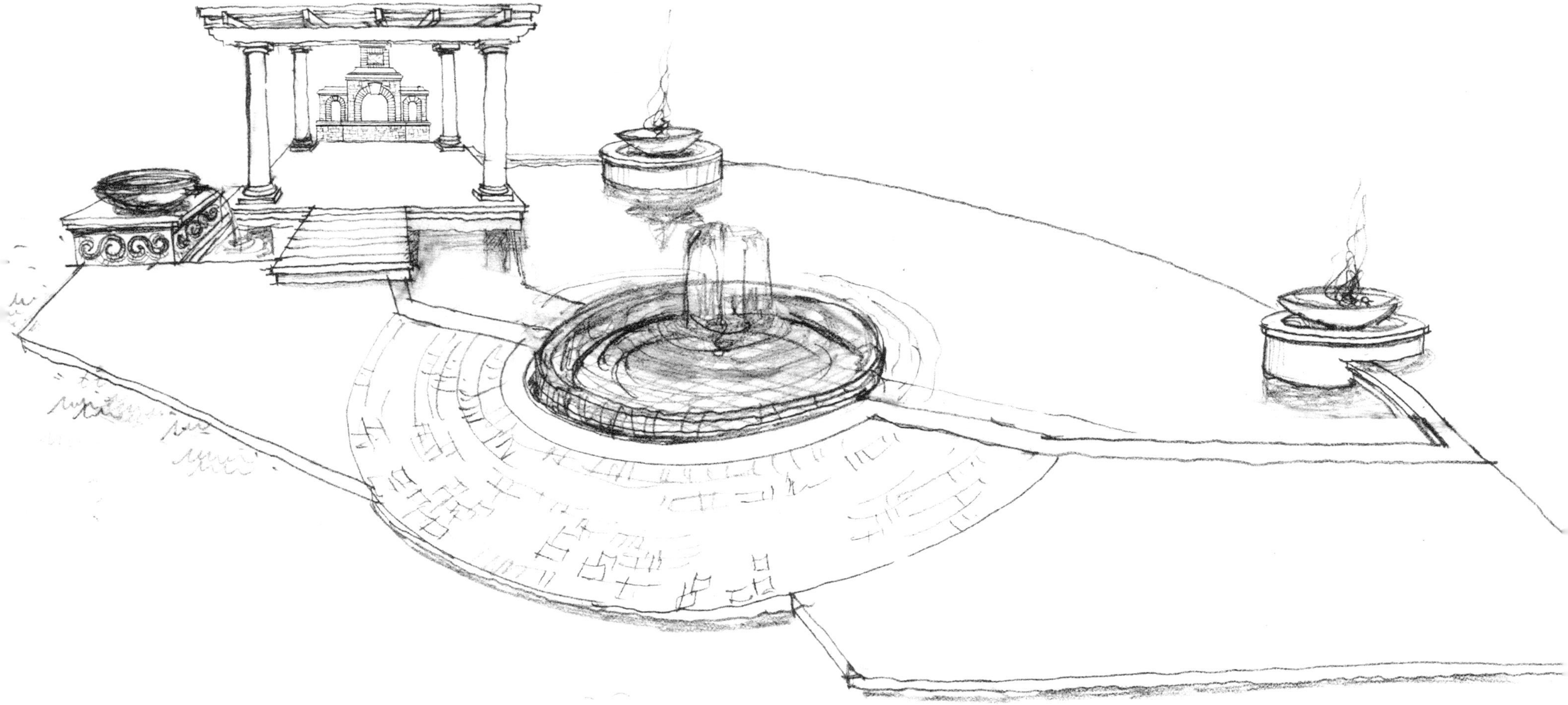

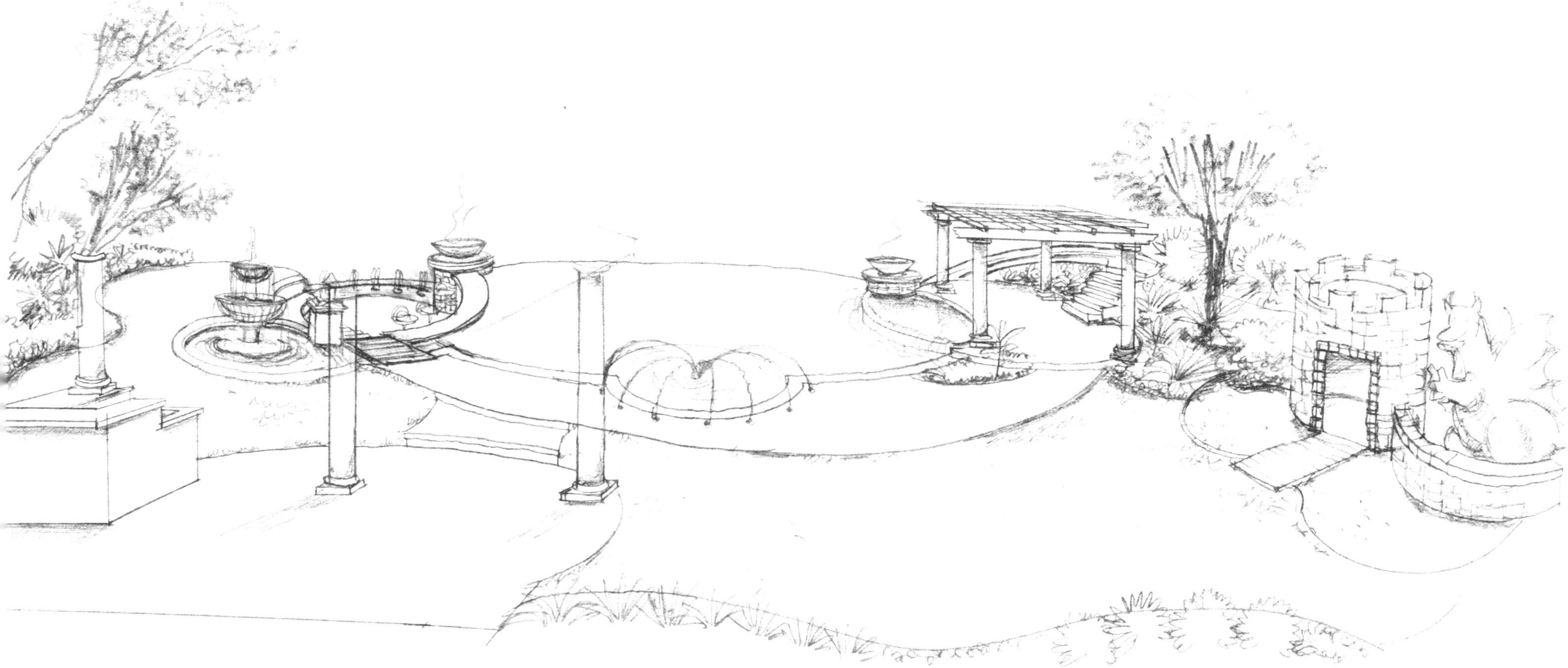

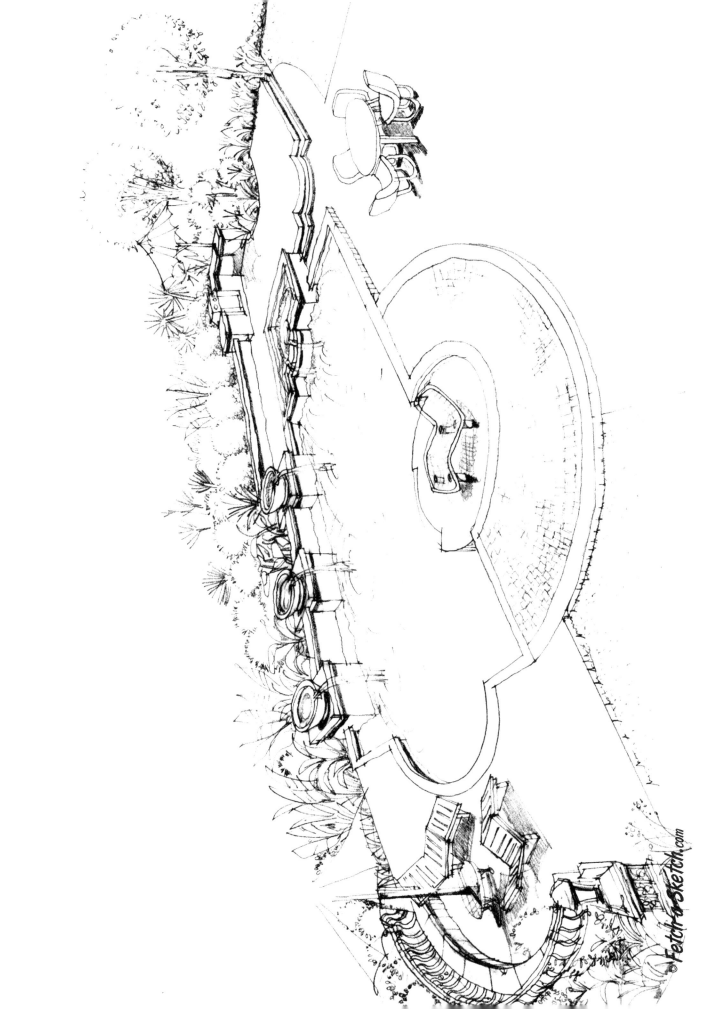

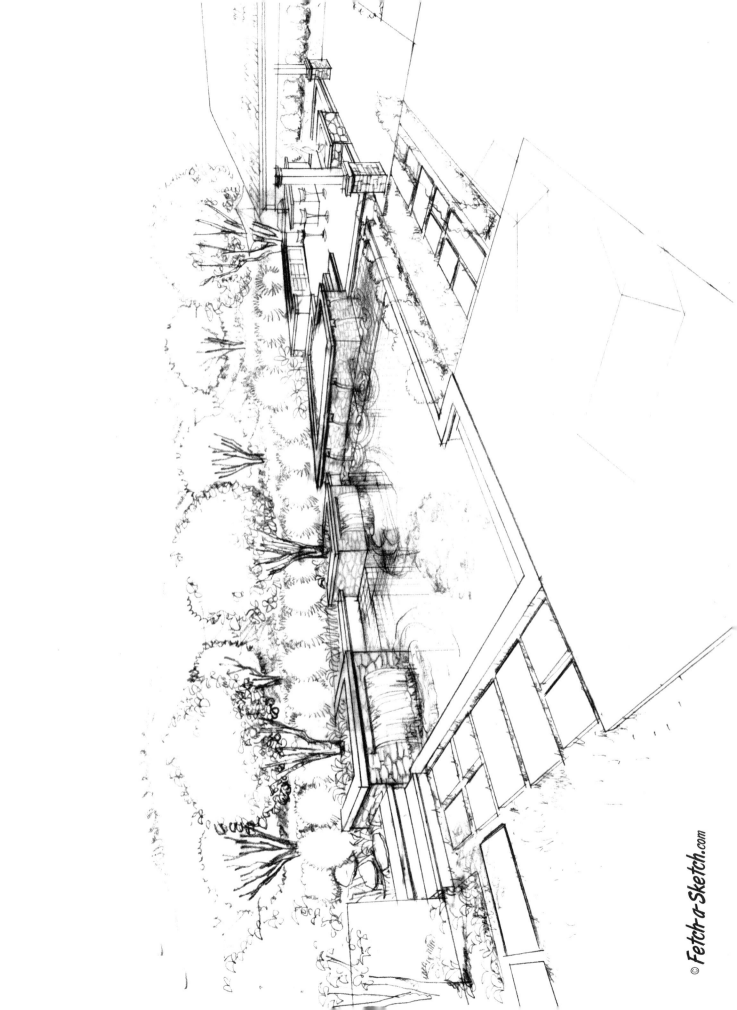

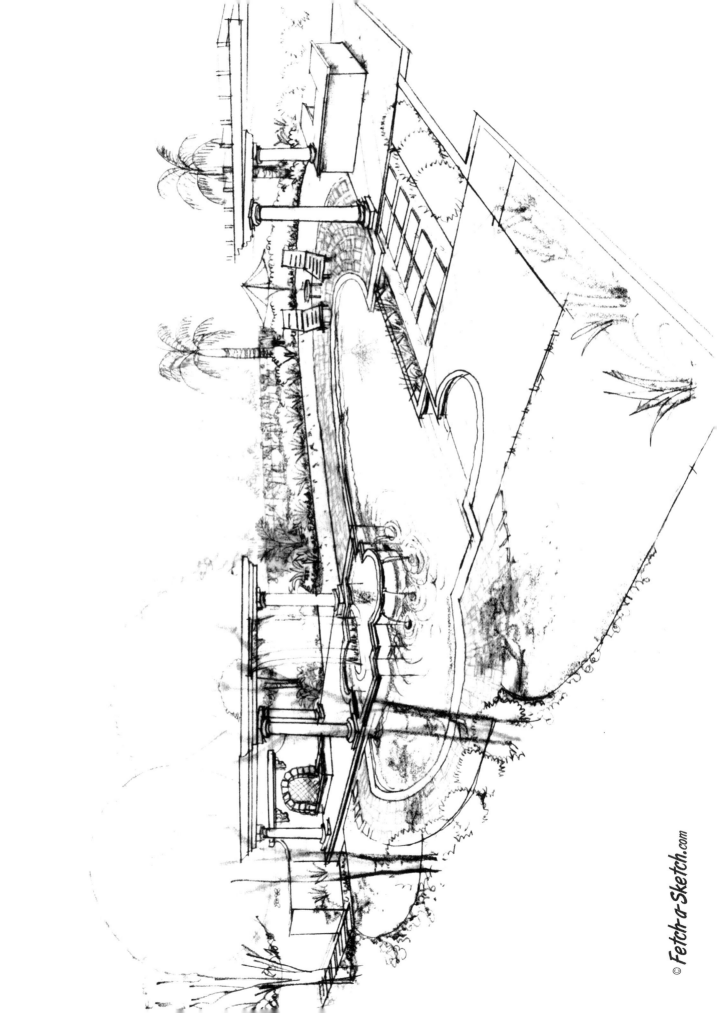

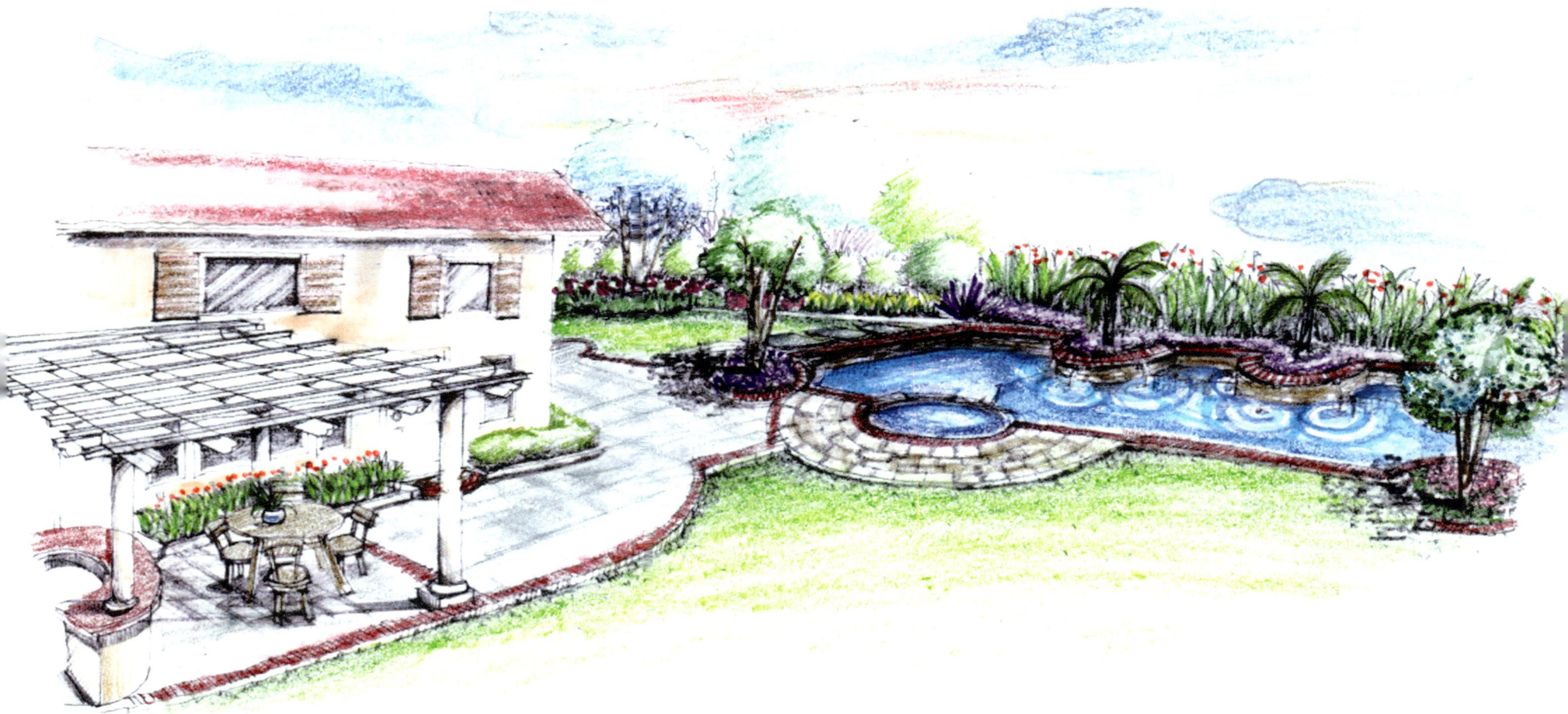

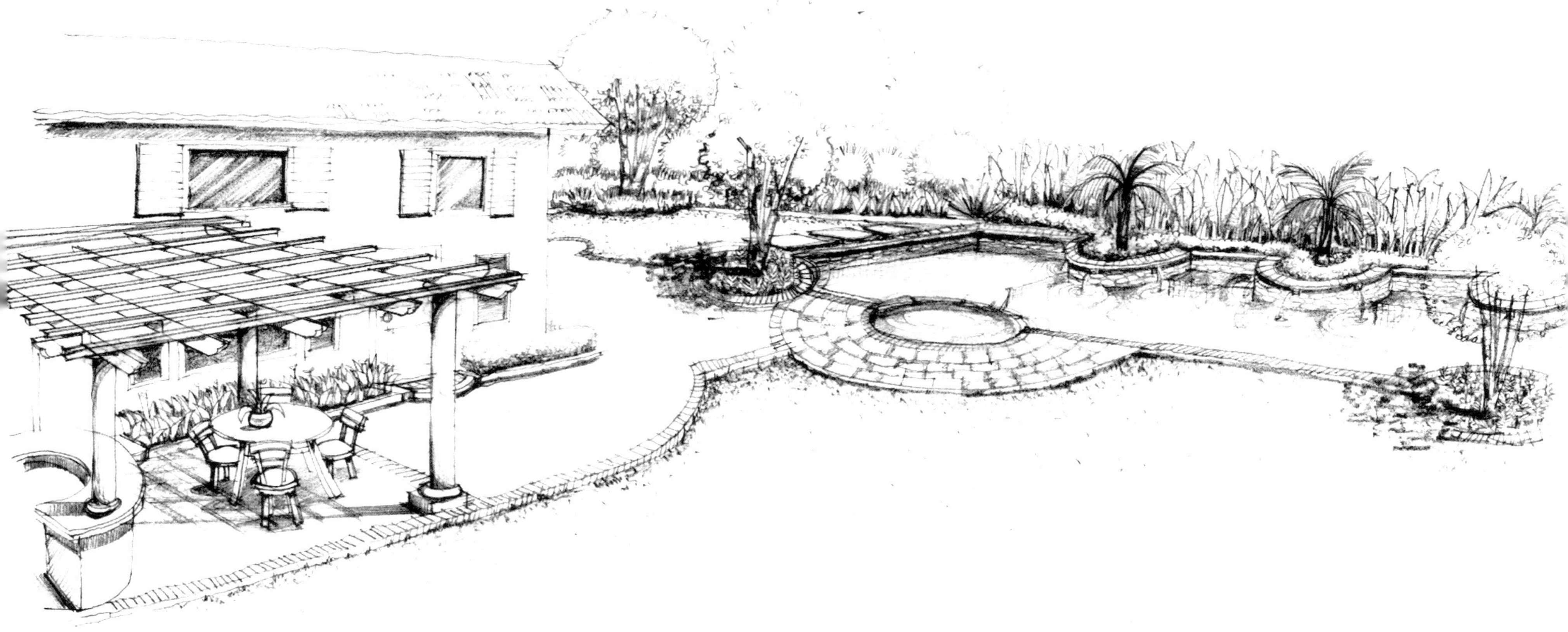

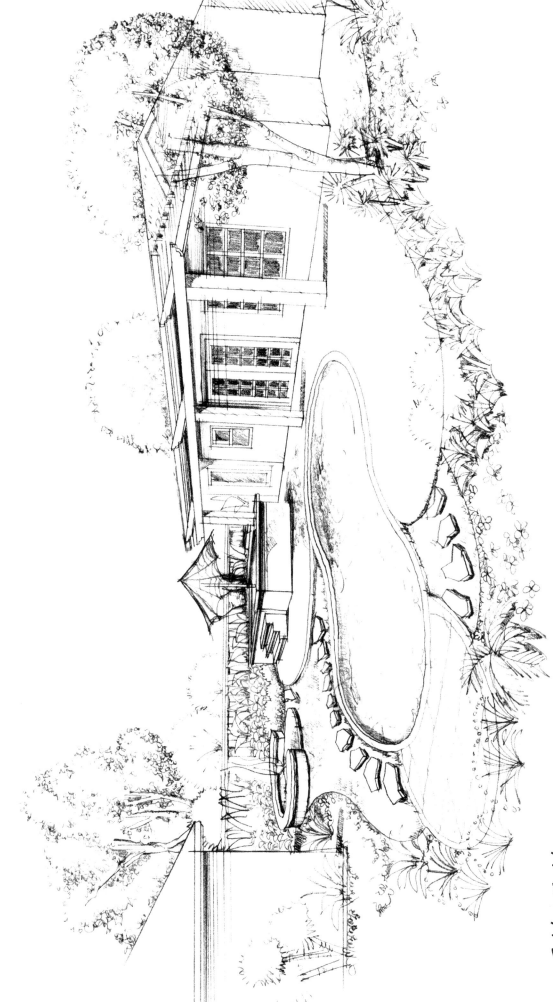

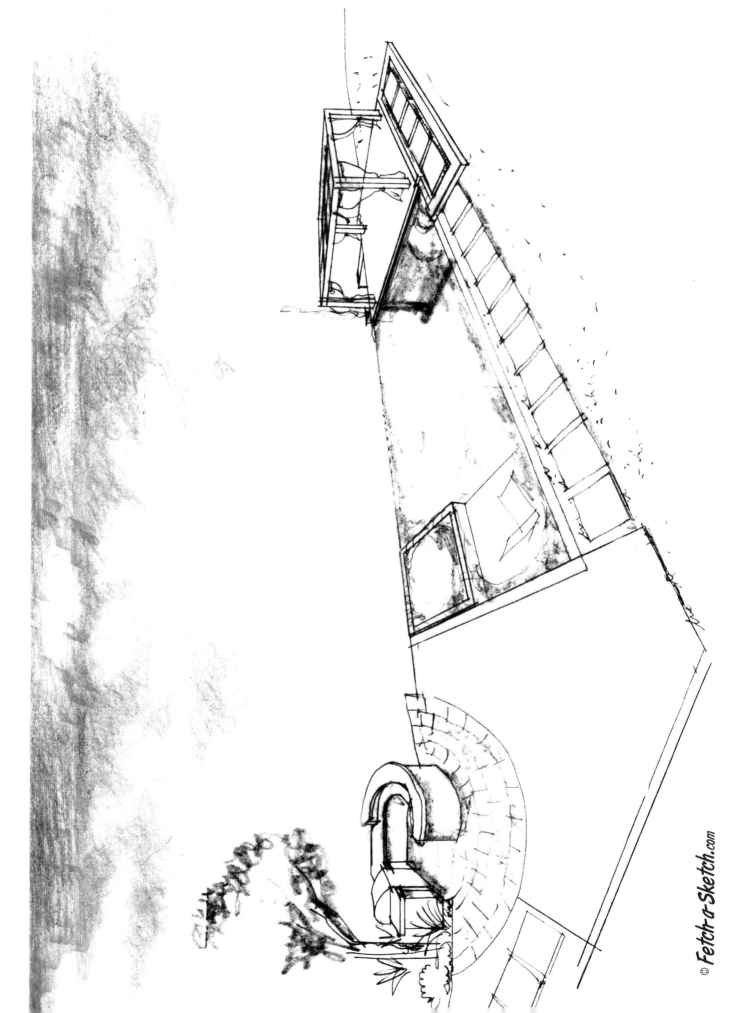

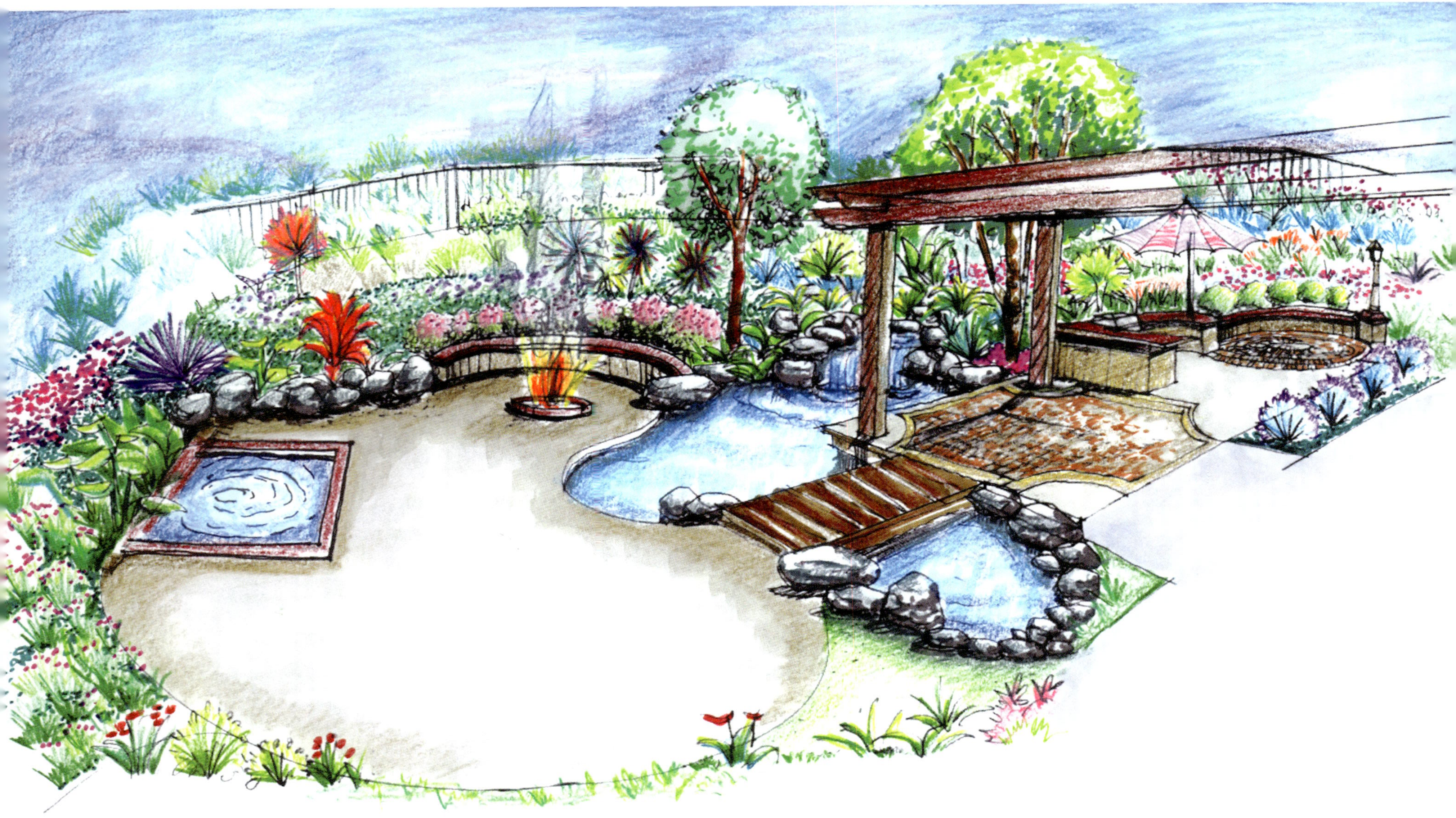

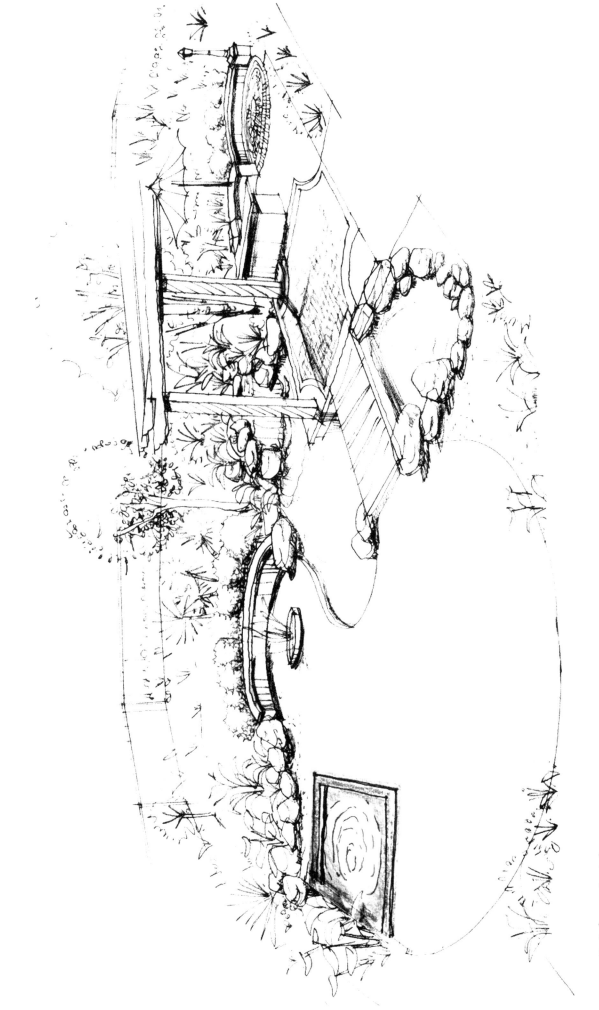

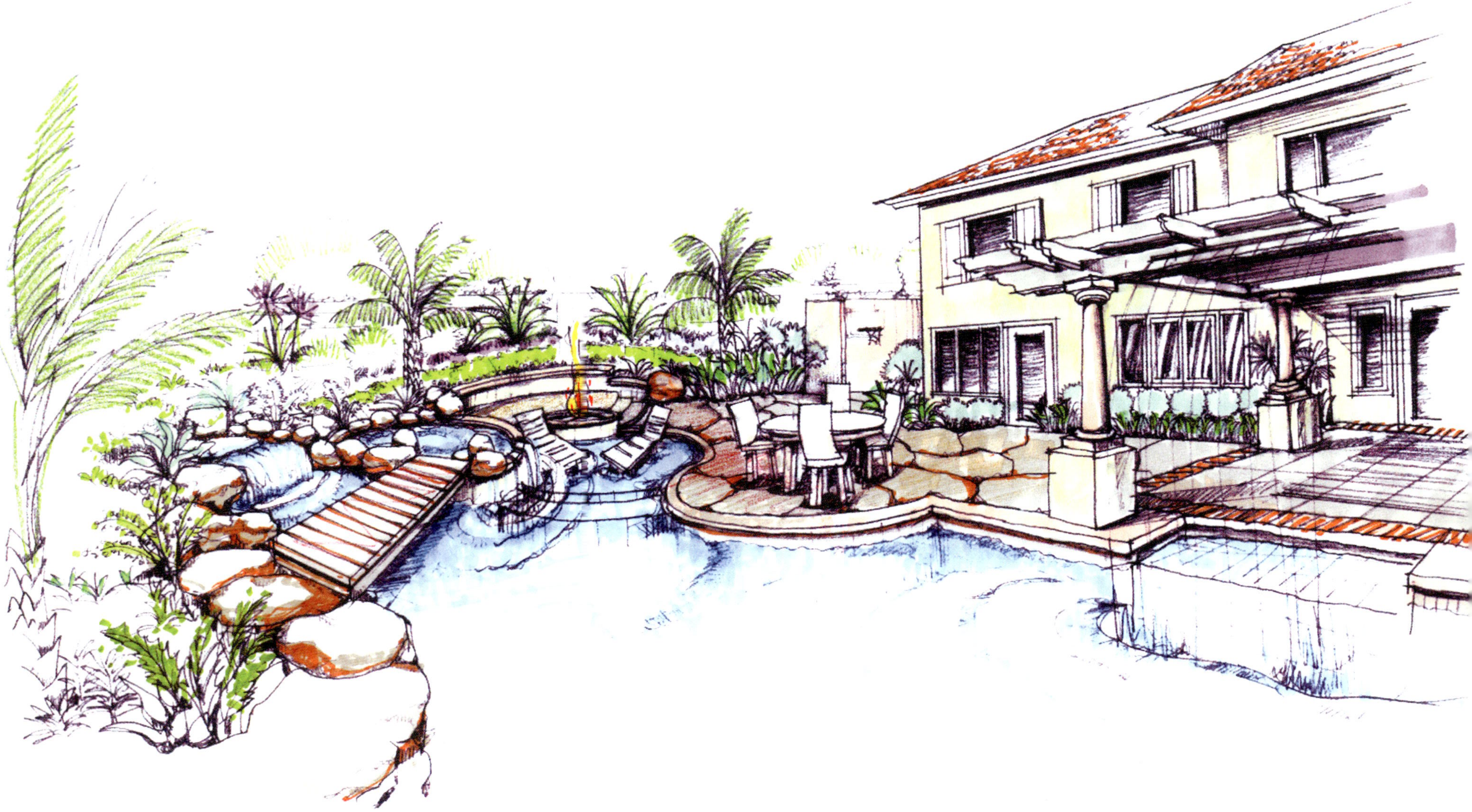

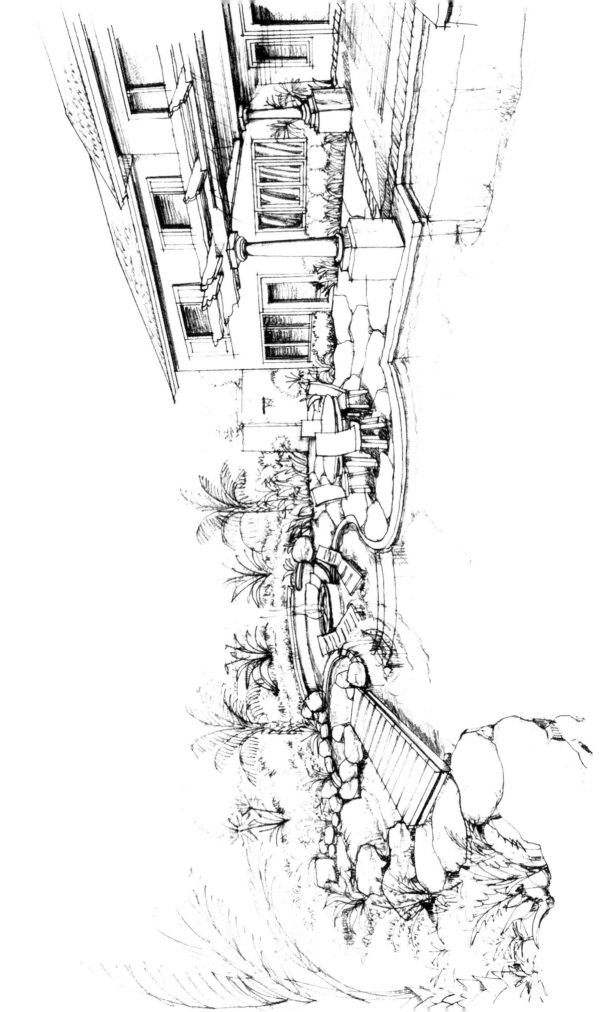

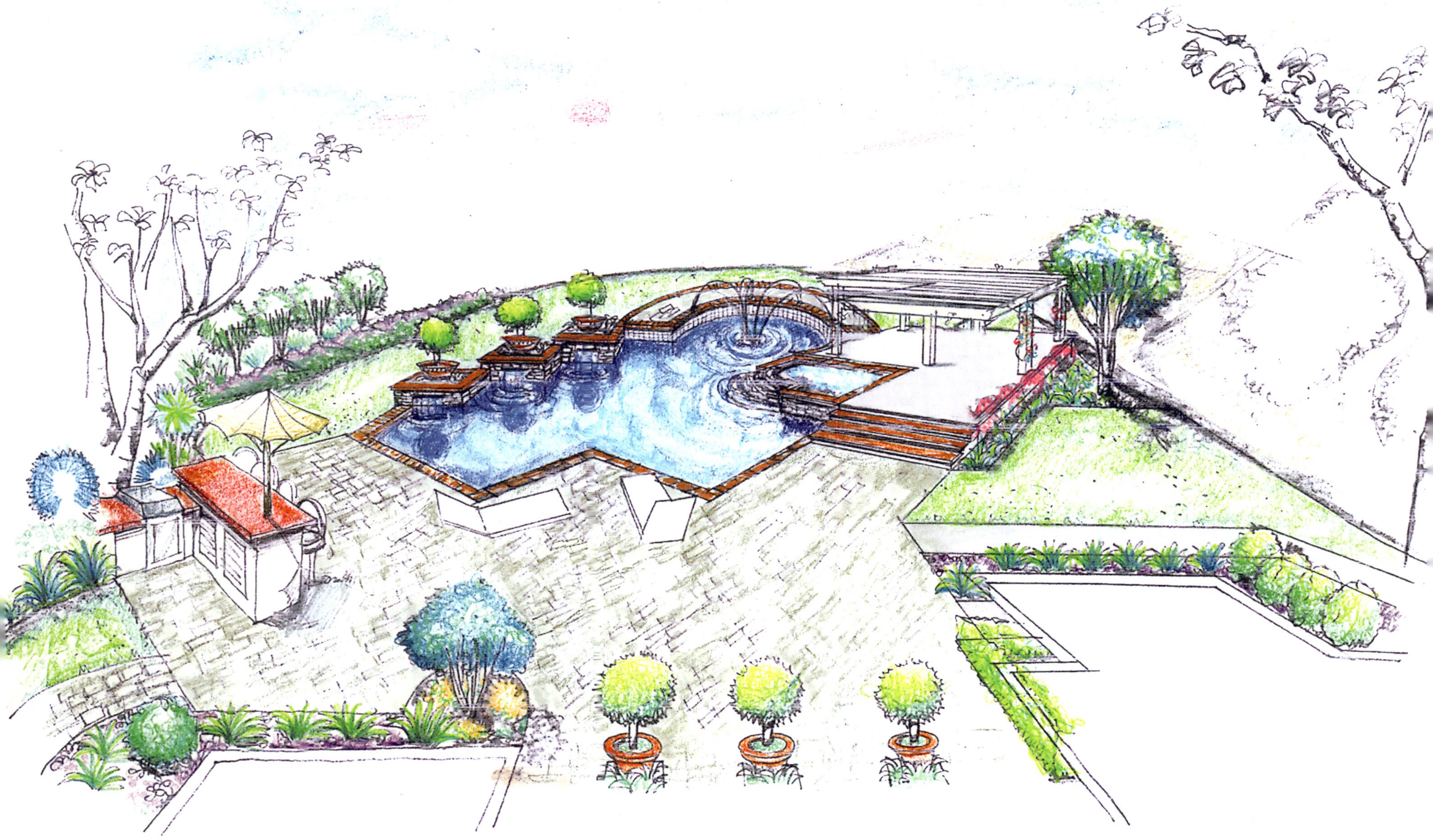

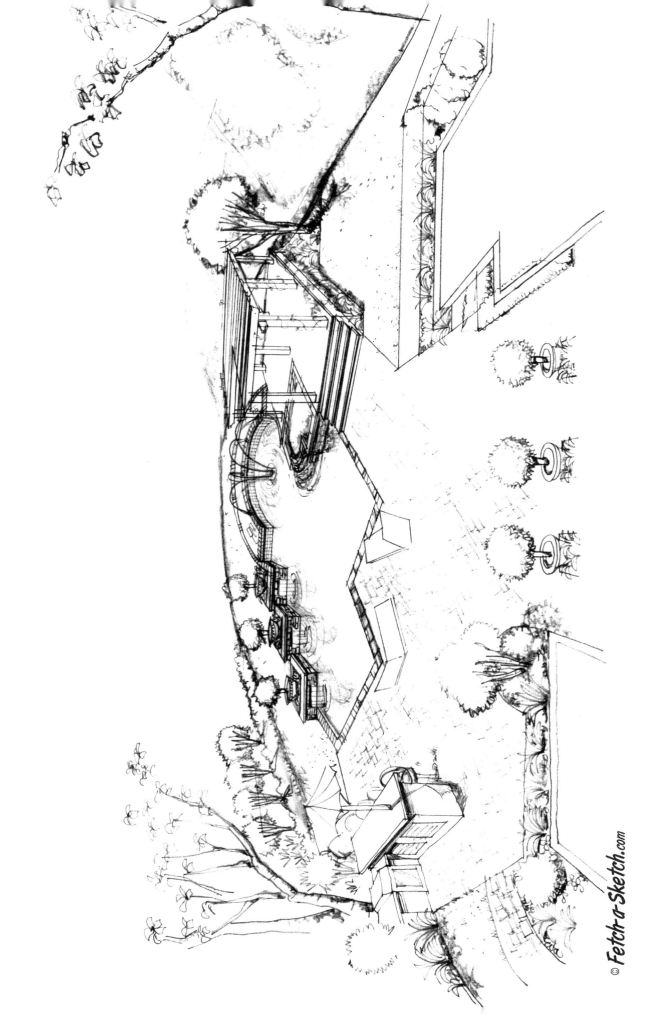

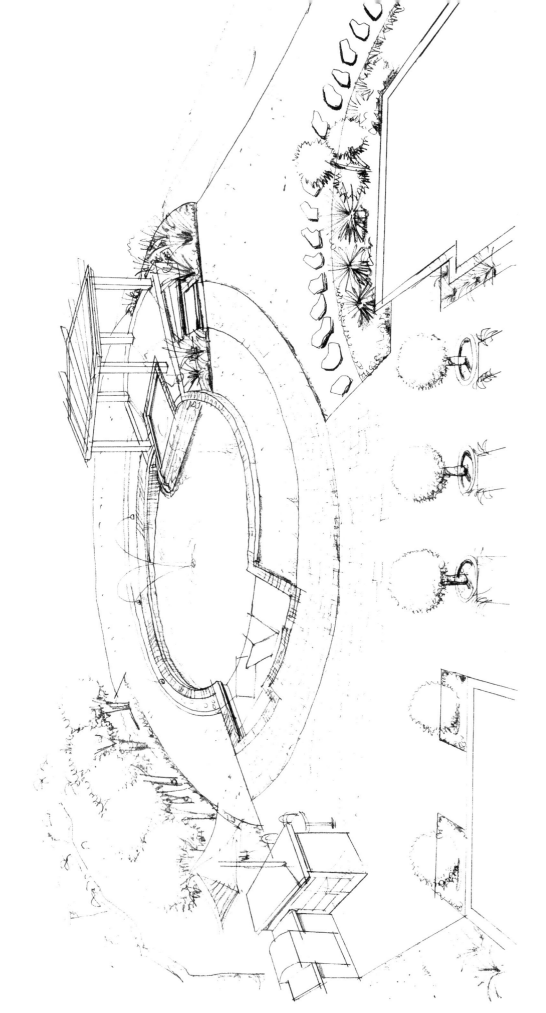

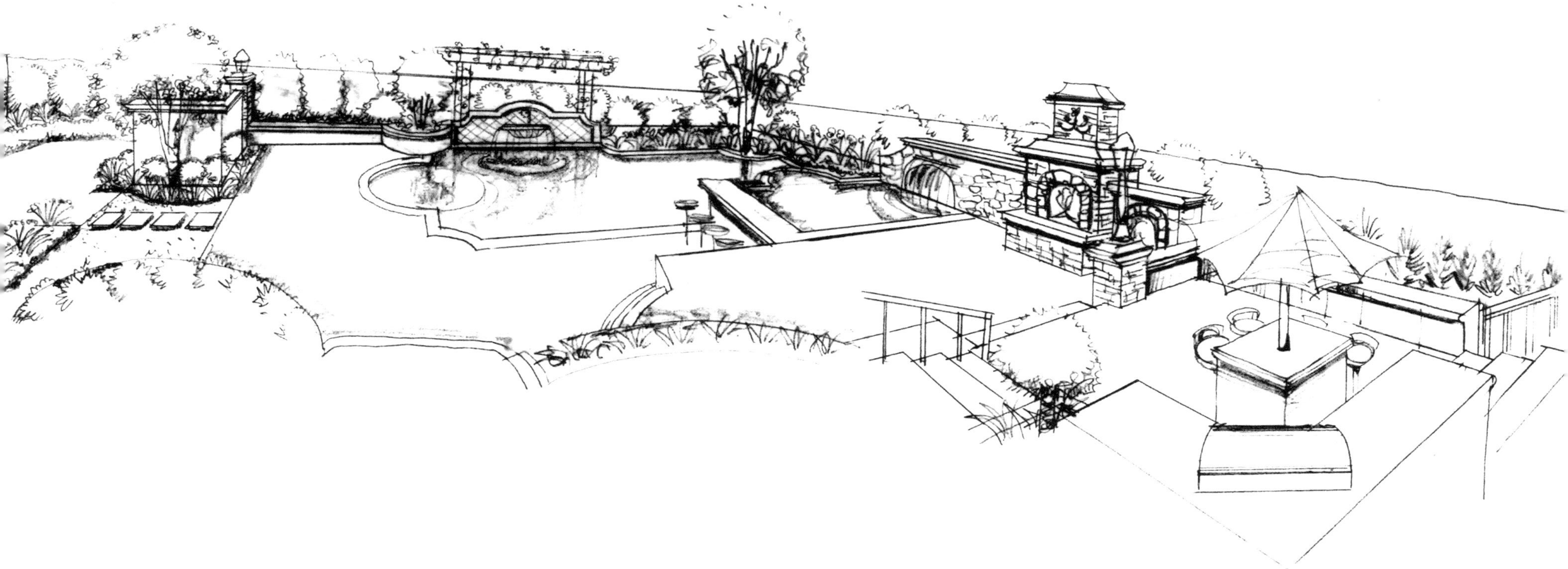

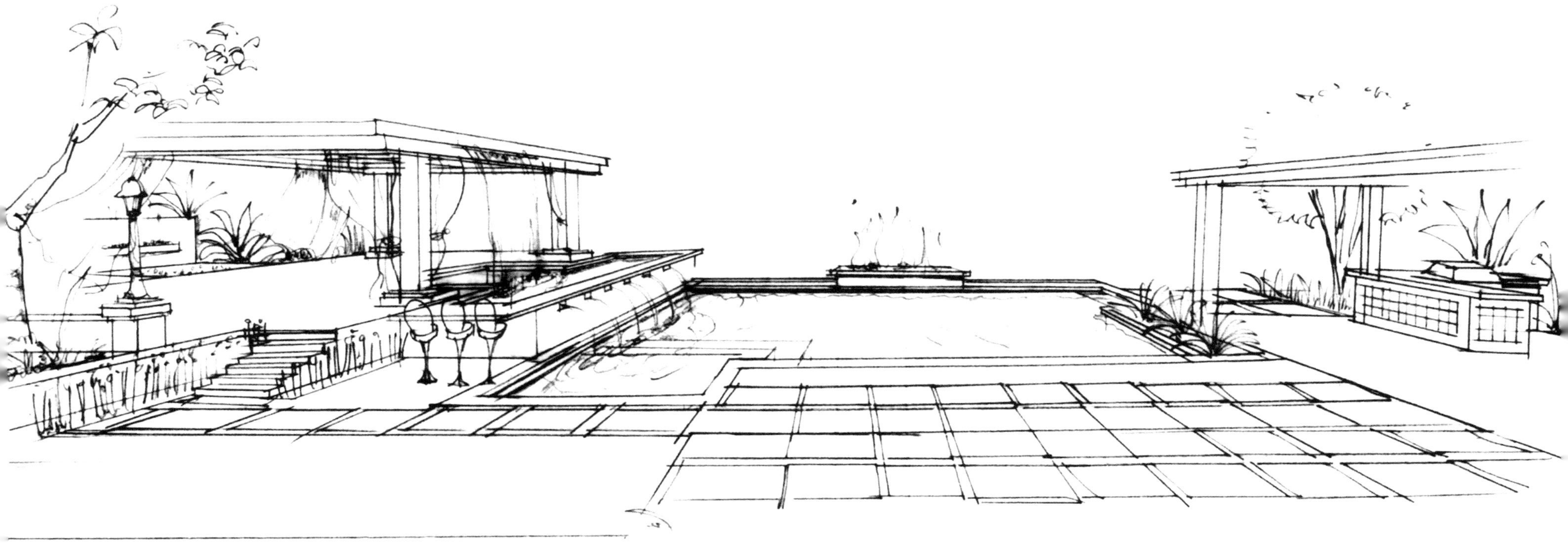

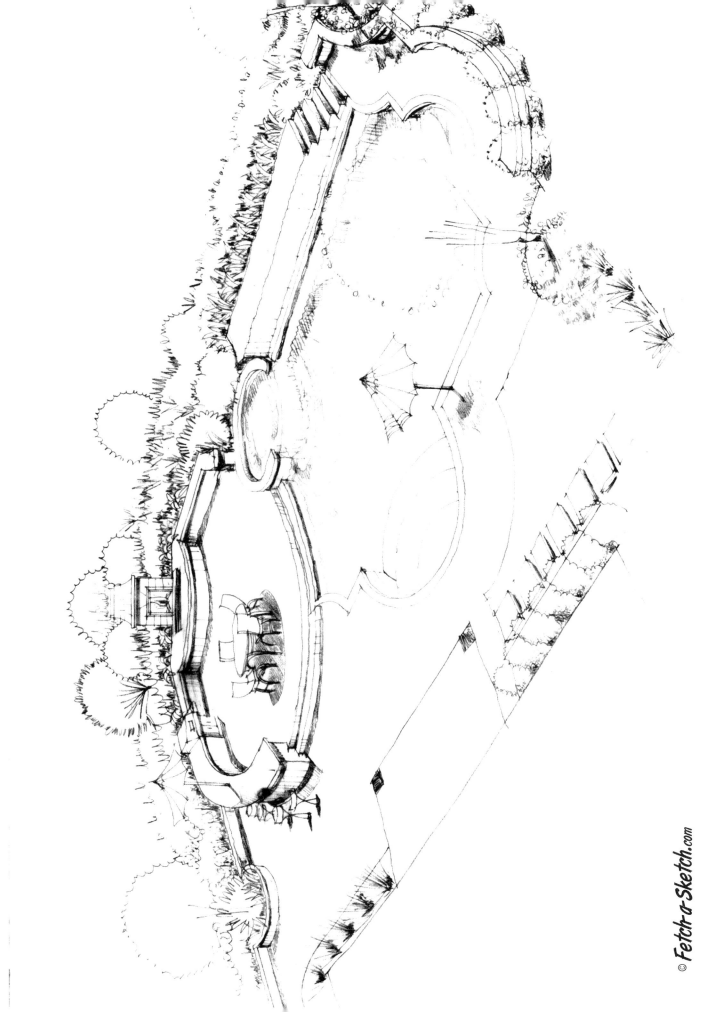

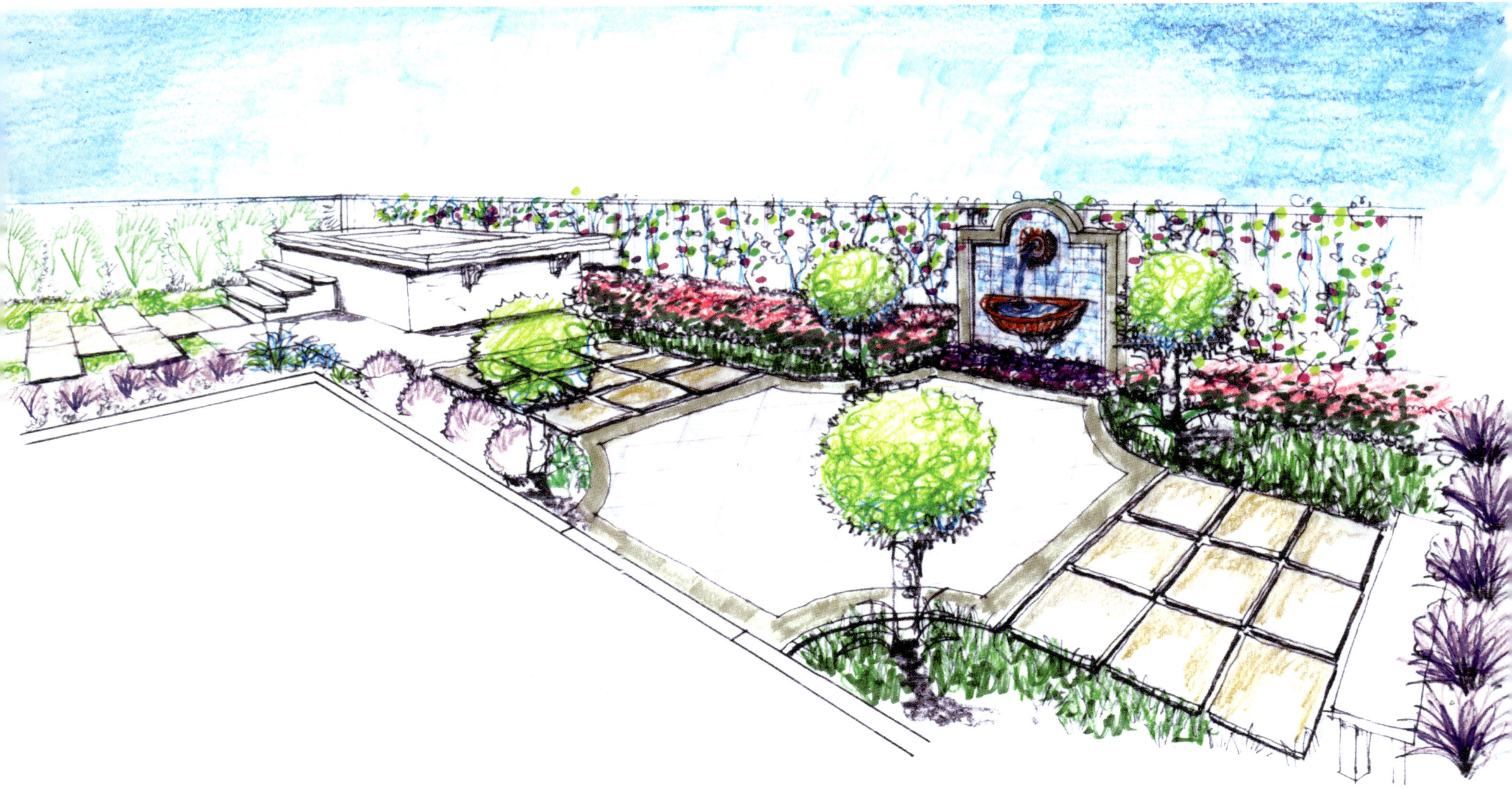

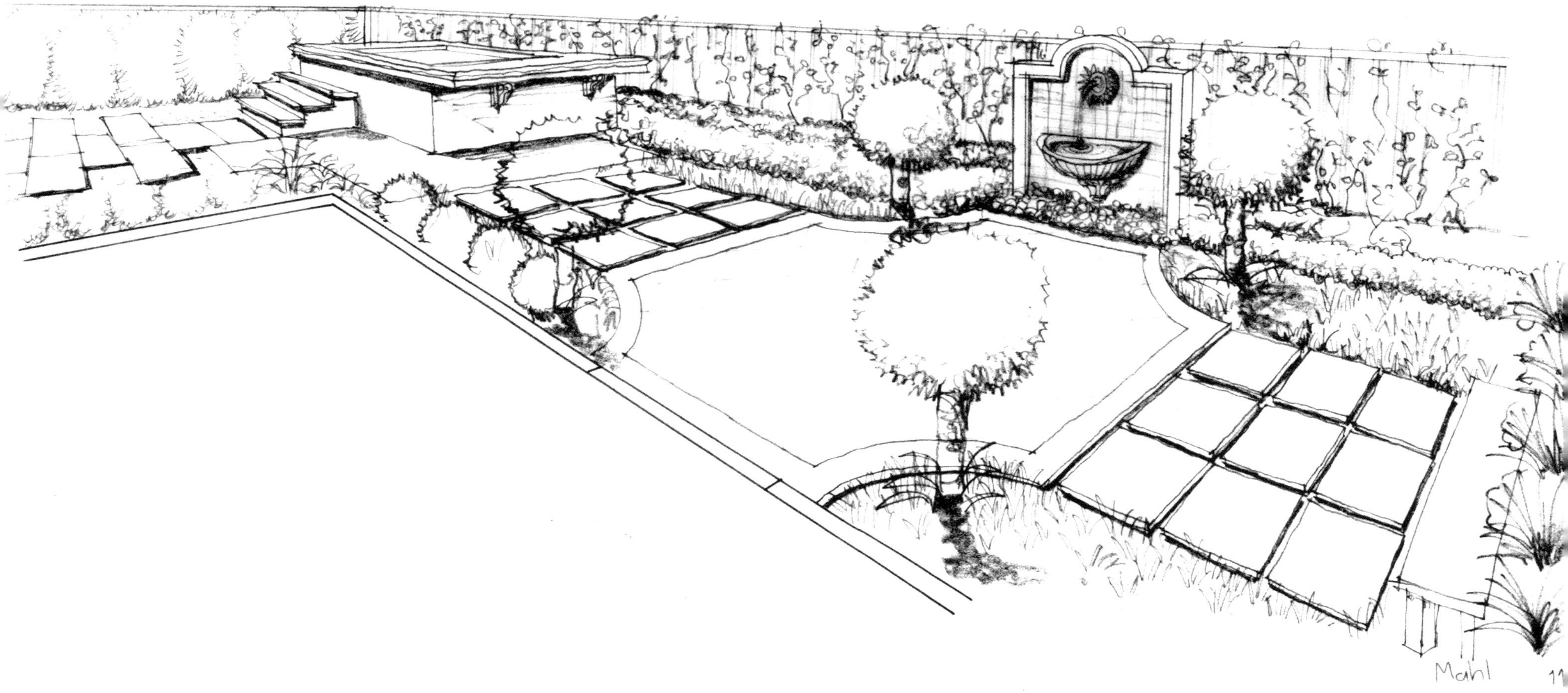
Mahl

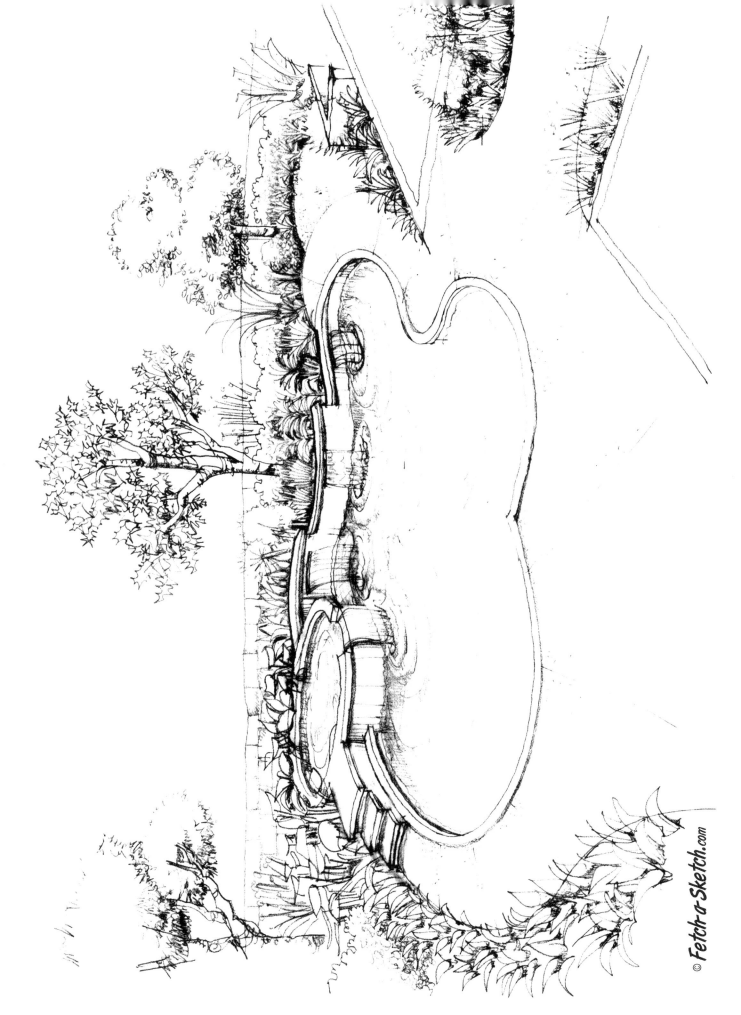

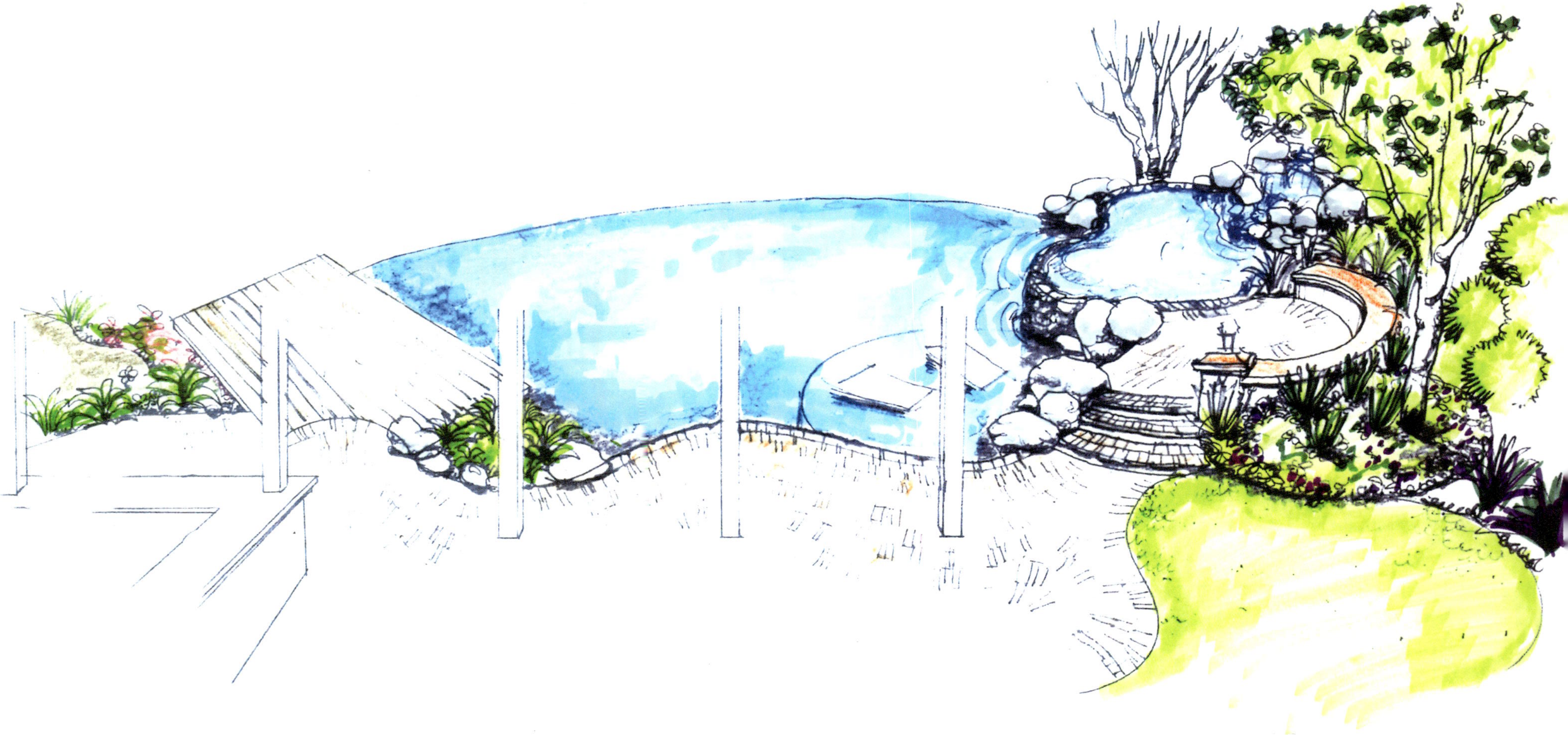

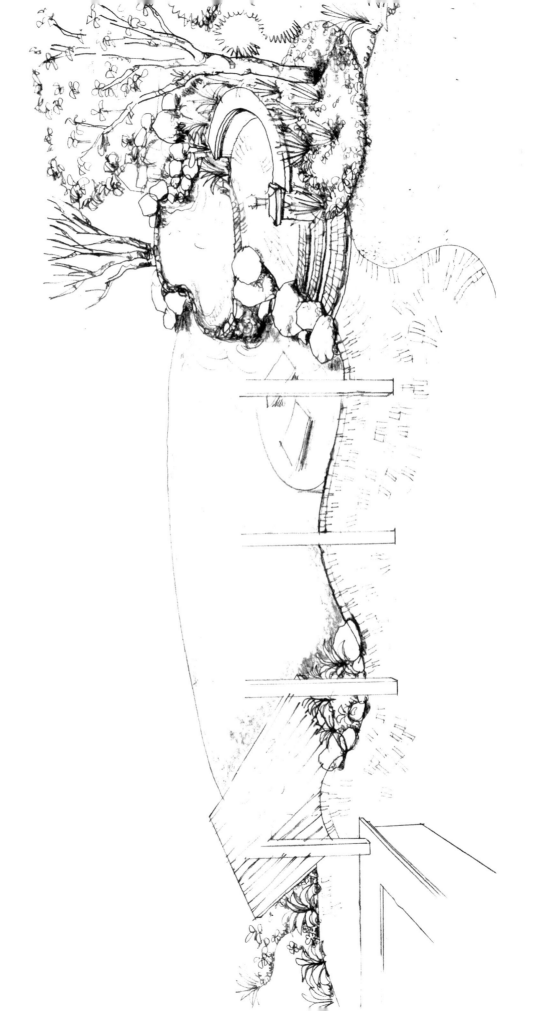

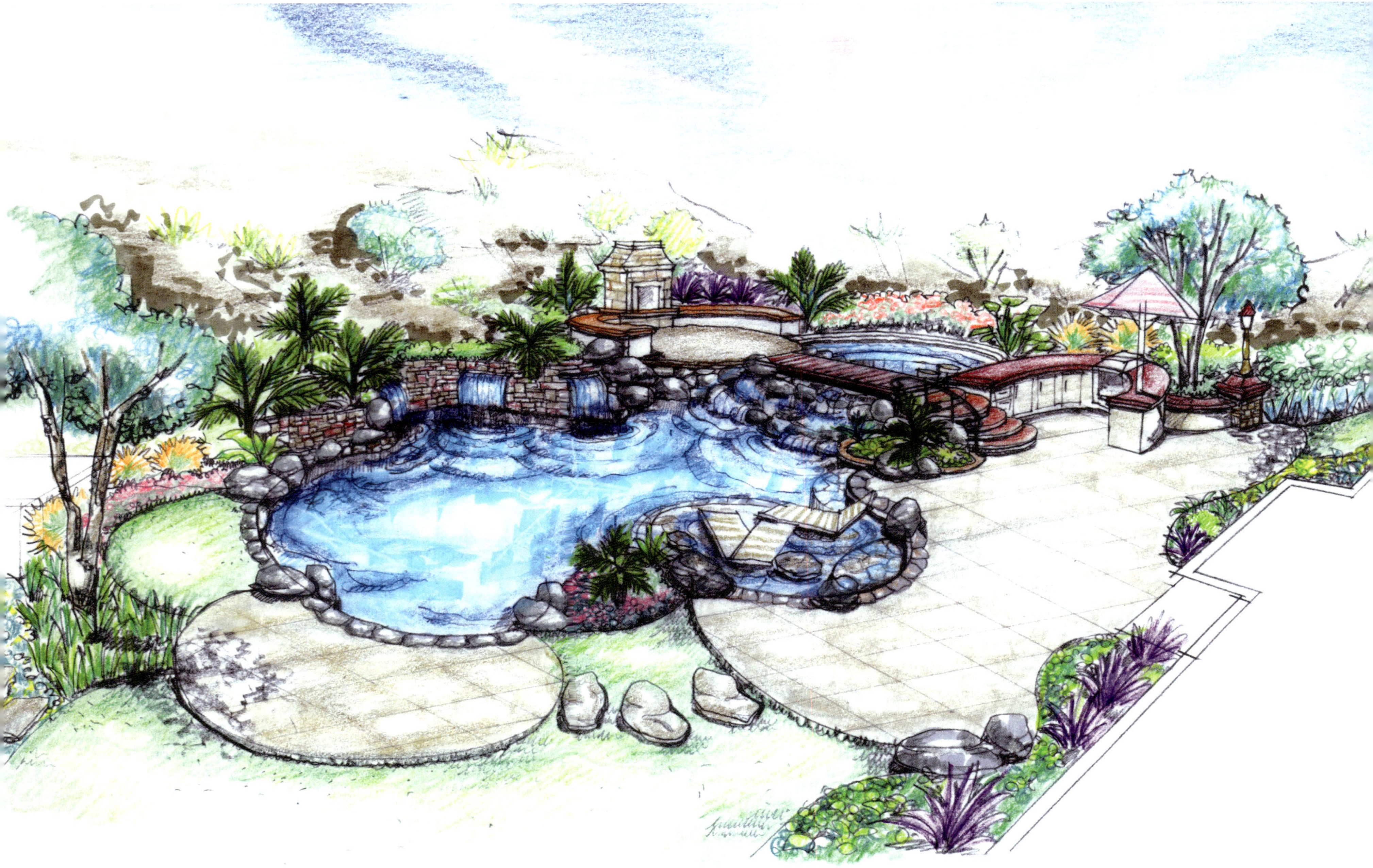
© Fetch-a-Sketch.com

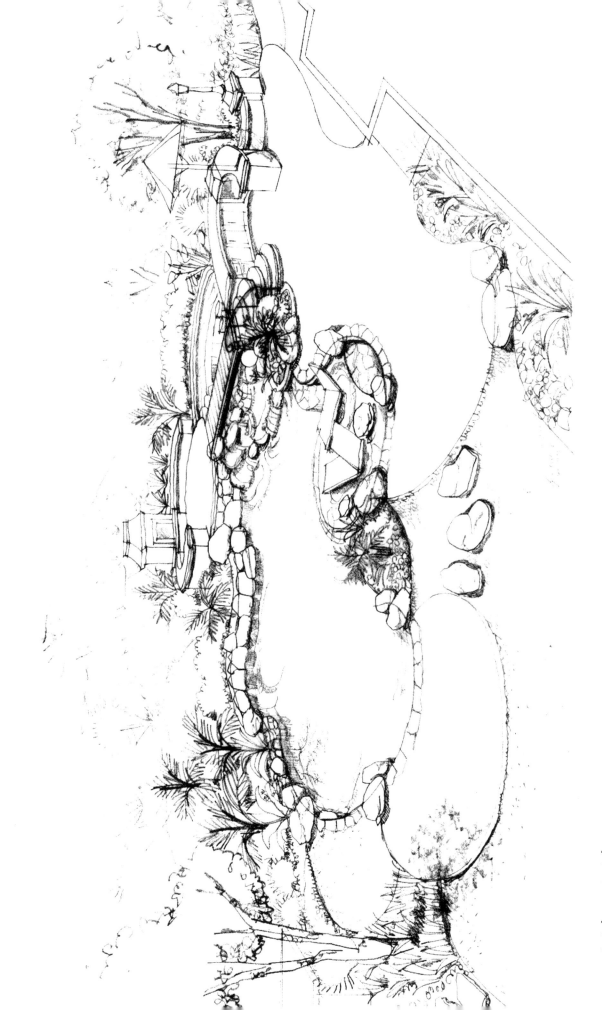

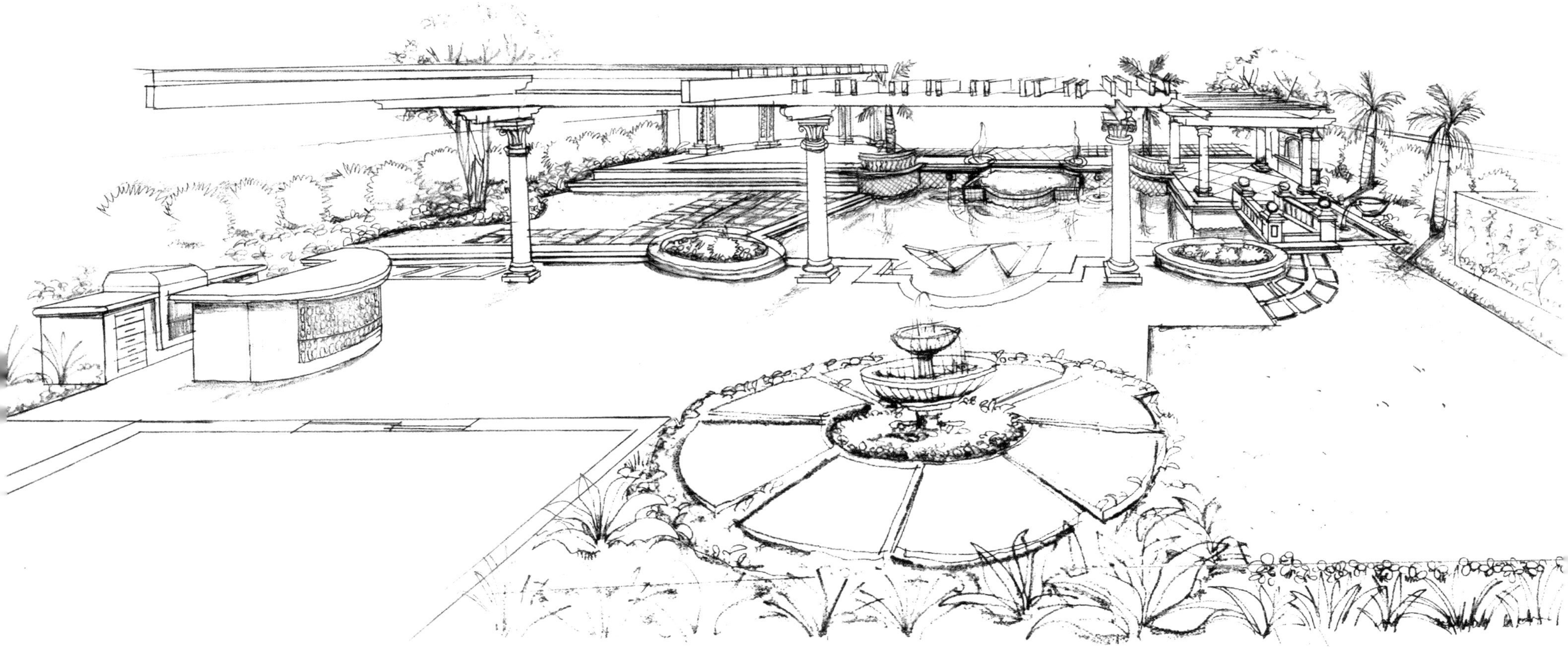

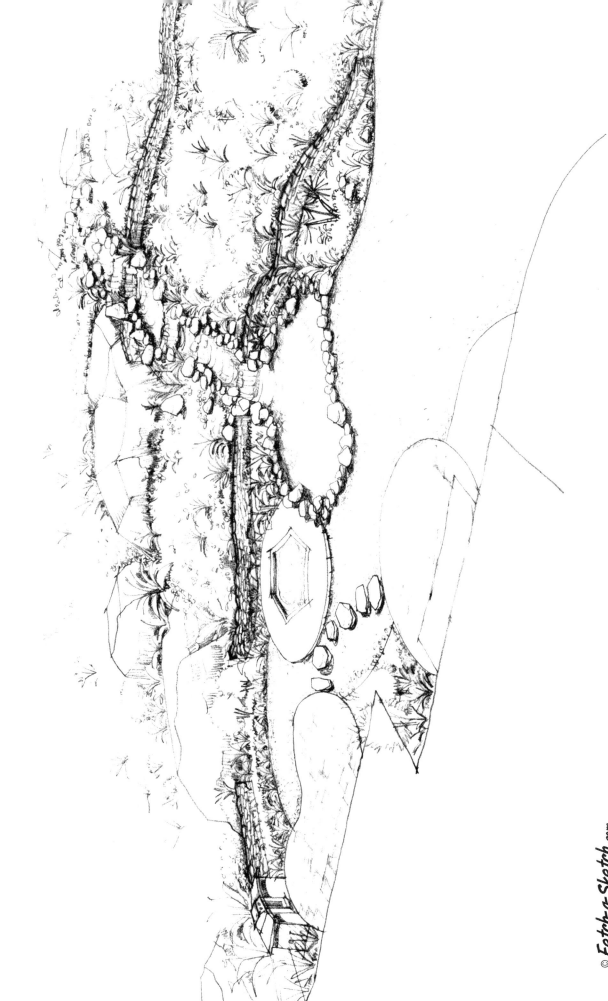

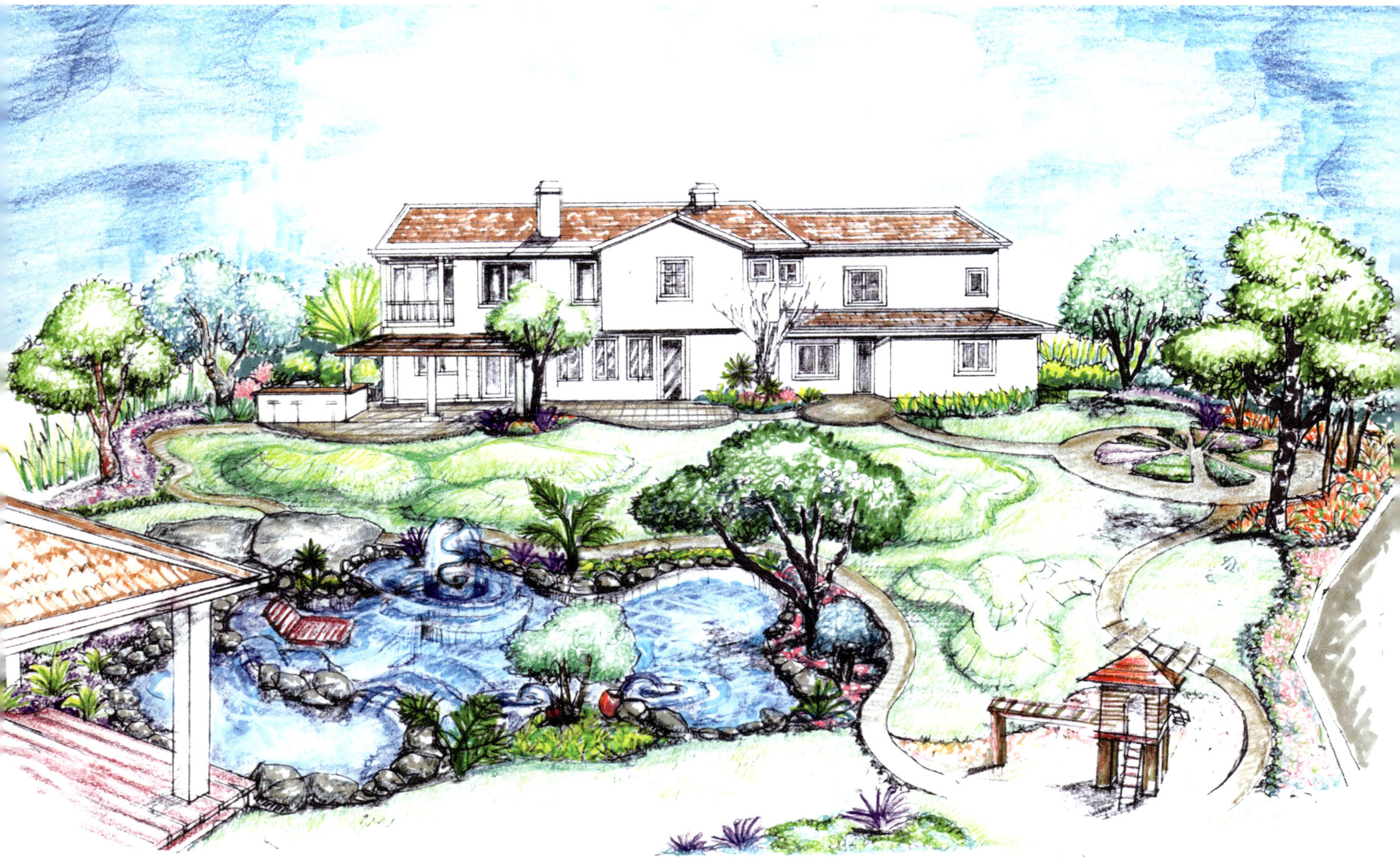

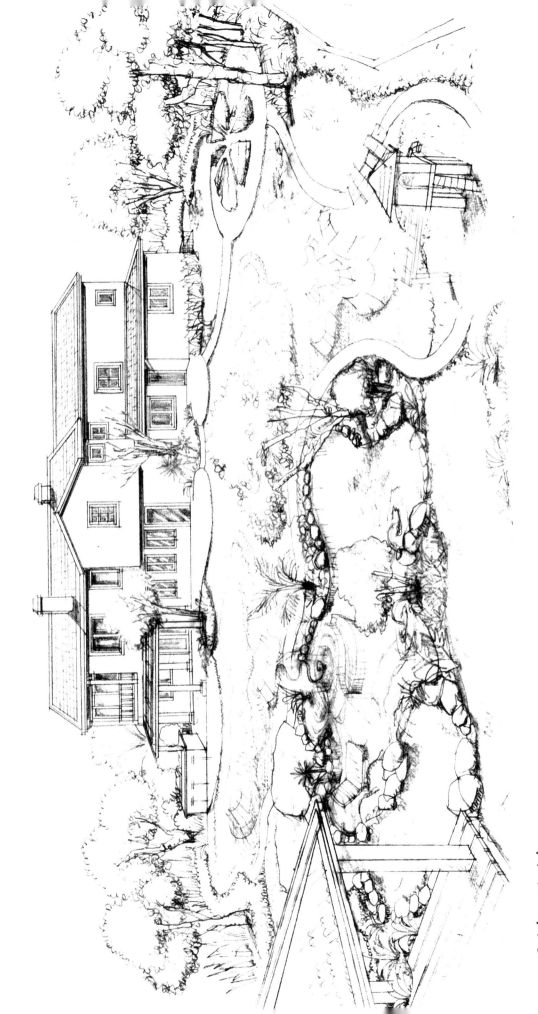

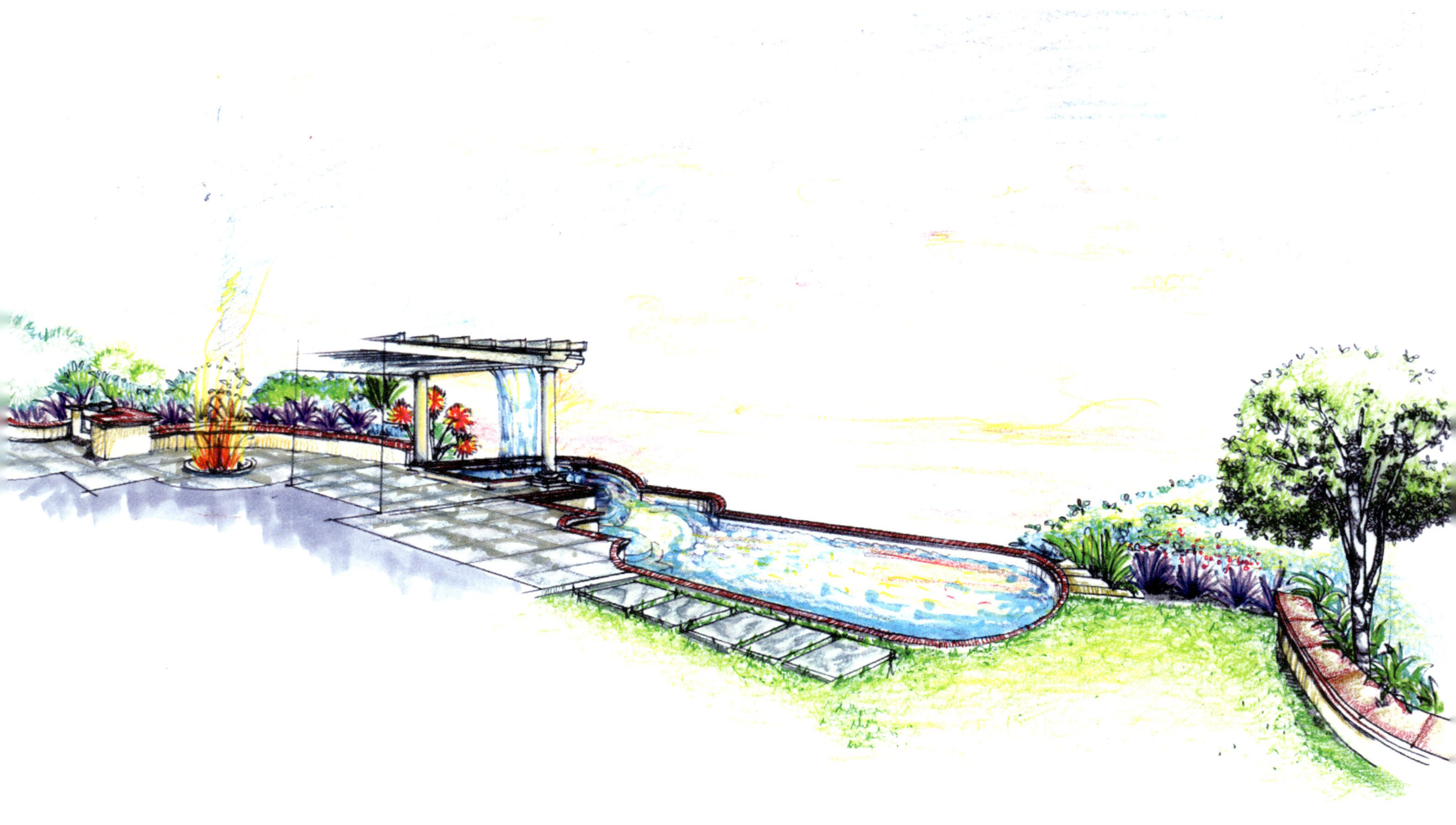

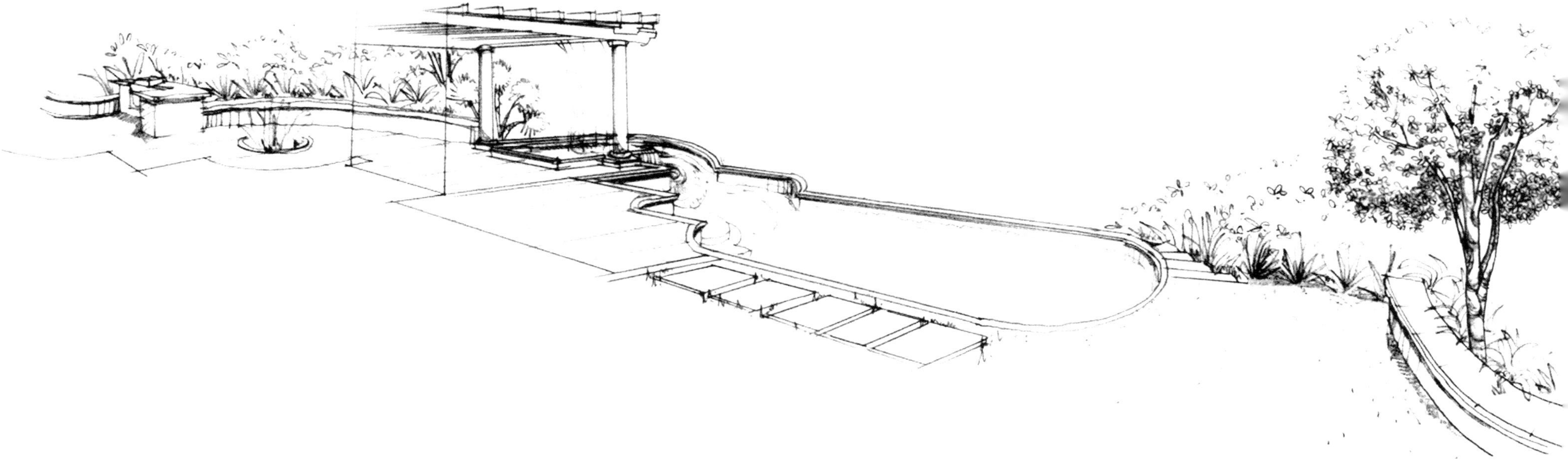

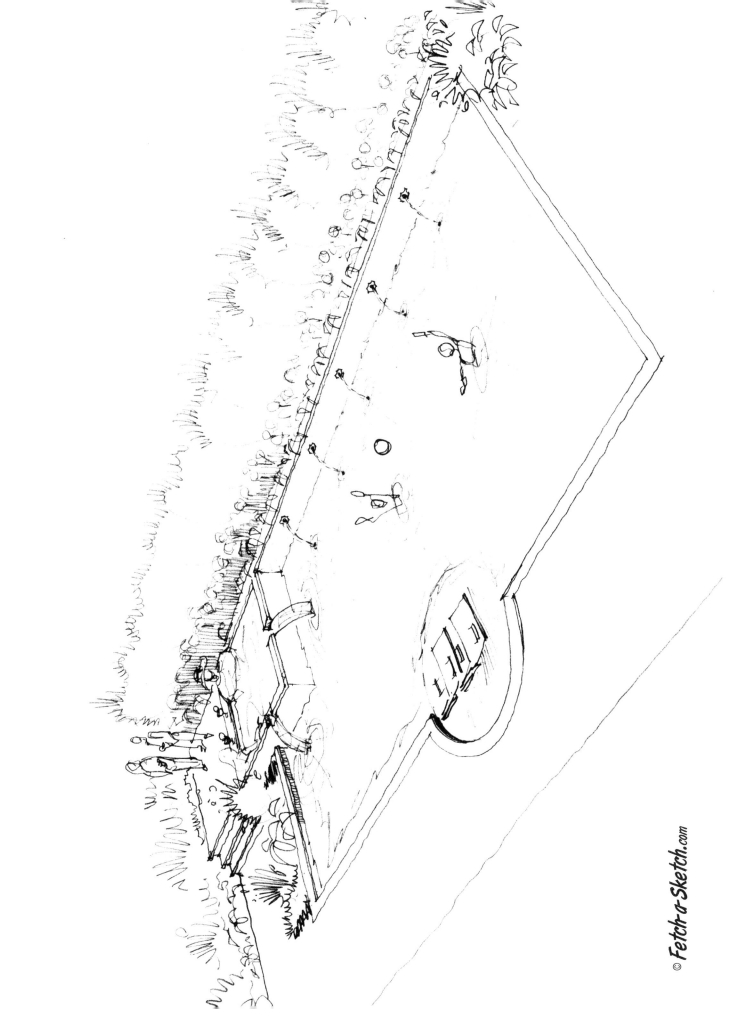

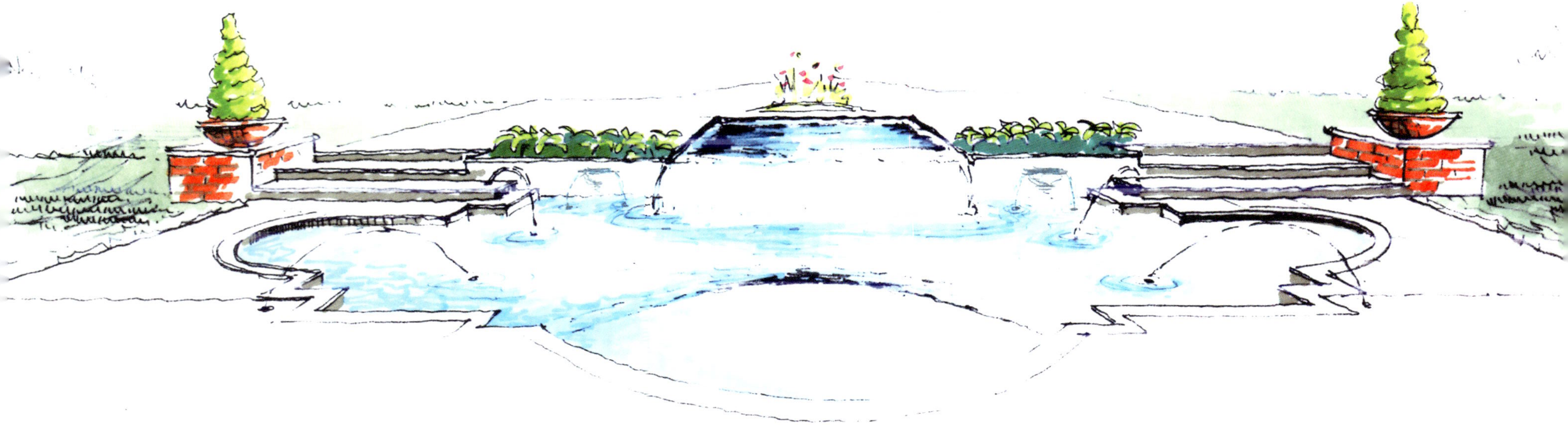

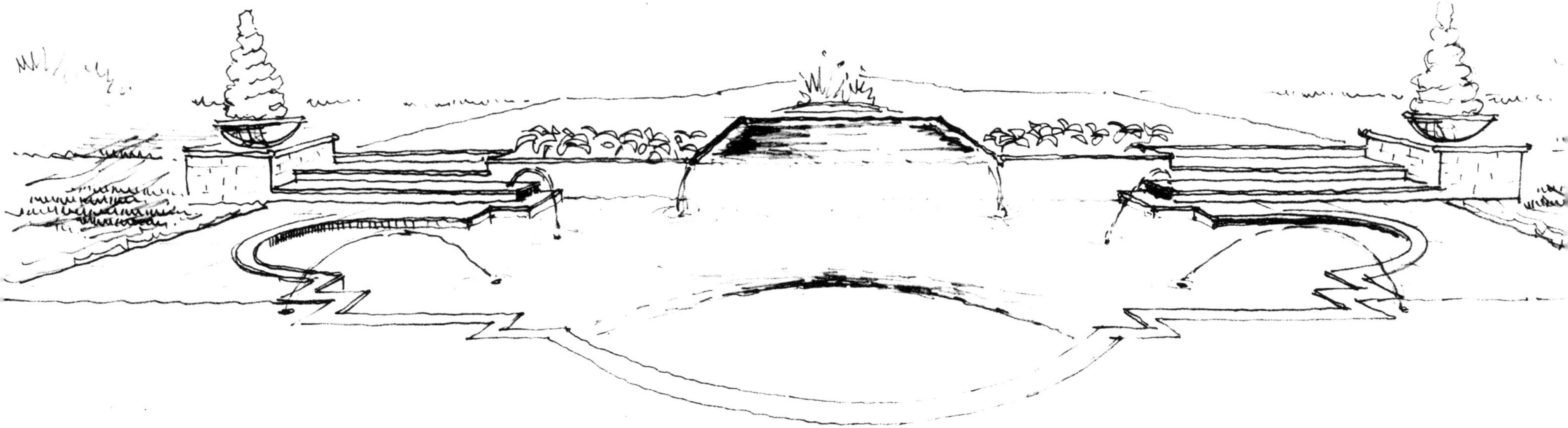

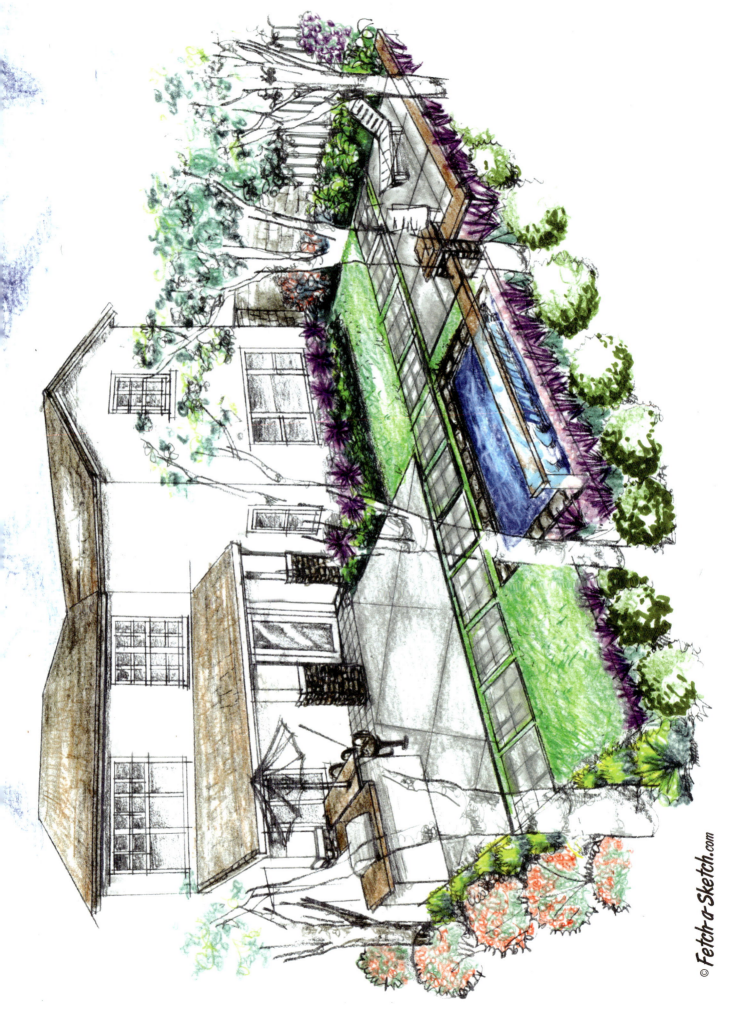

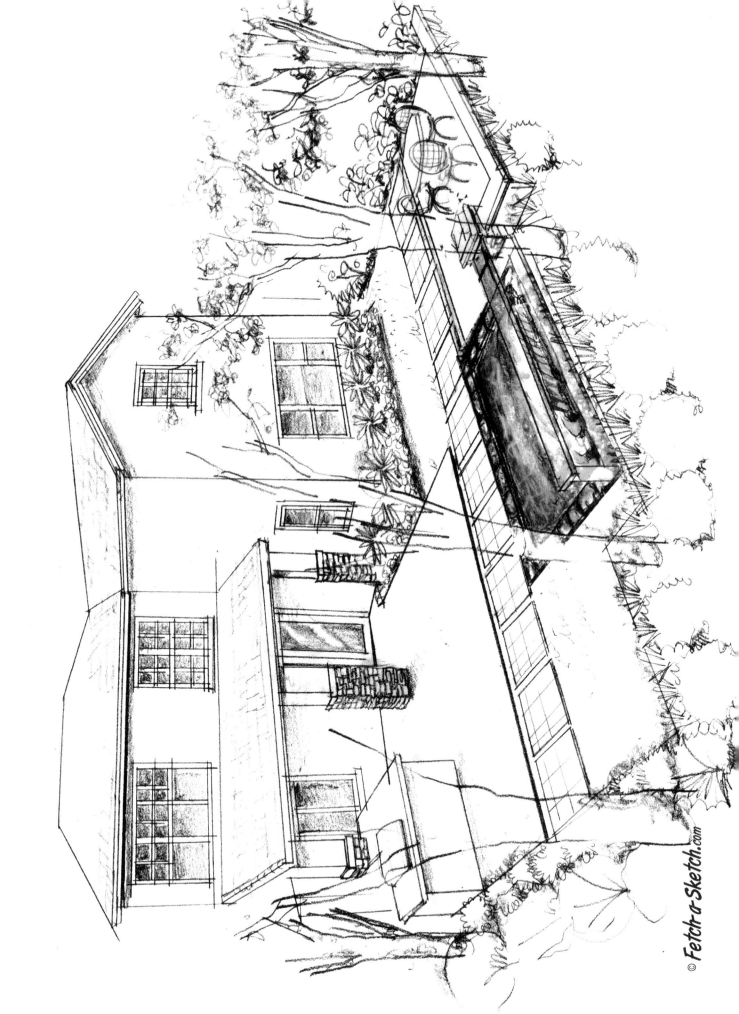

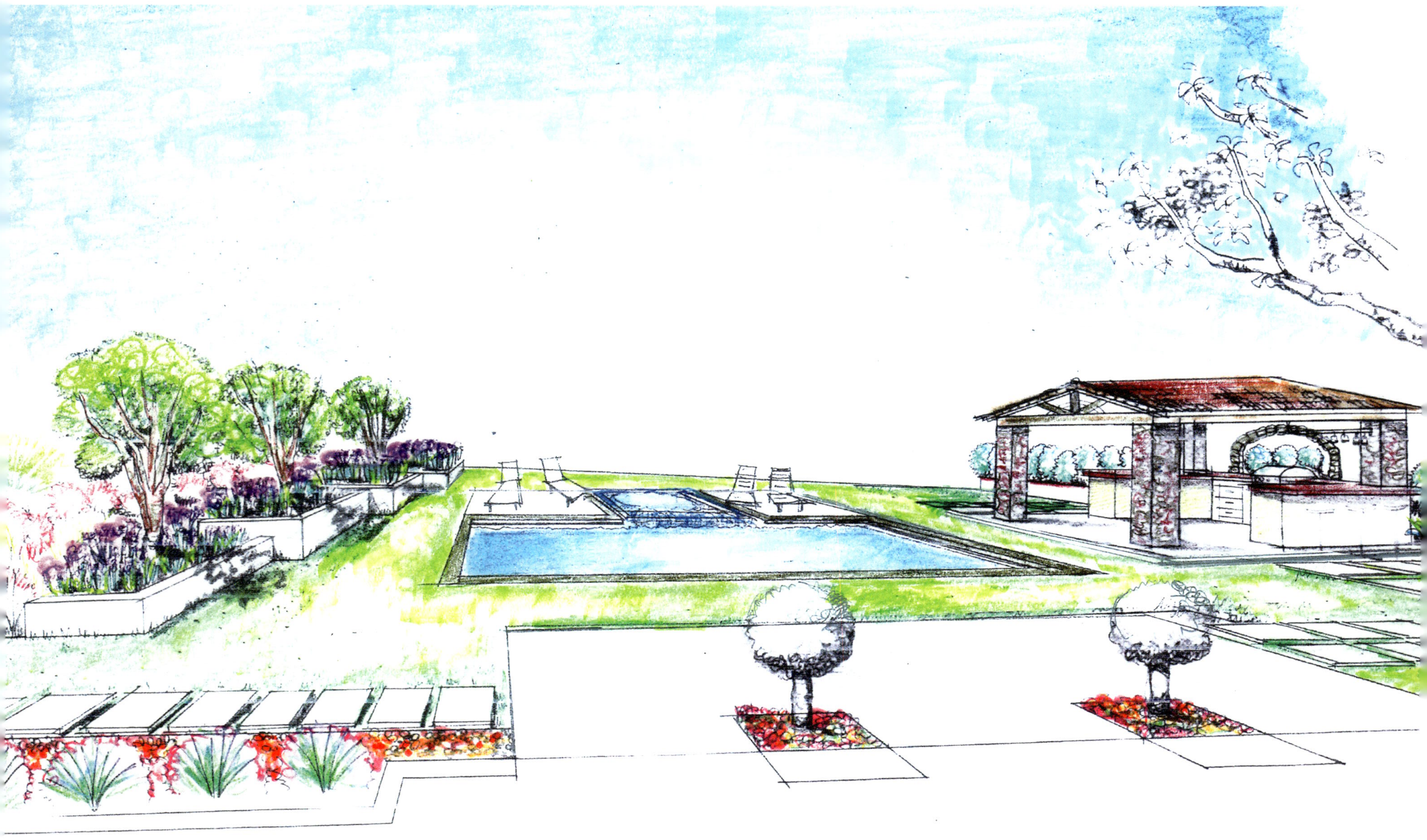

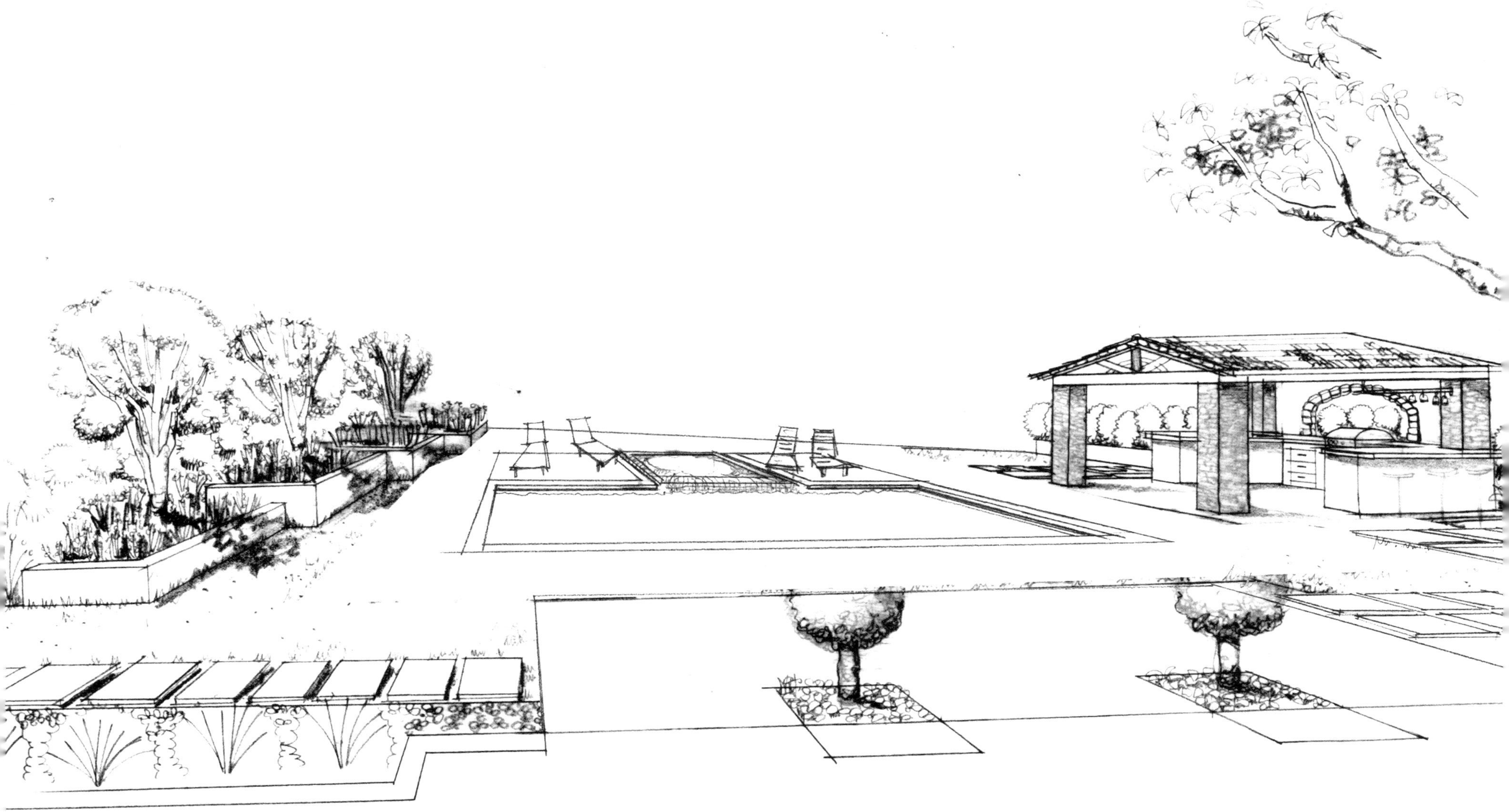

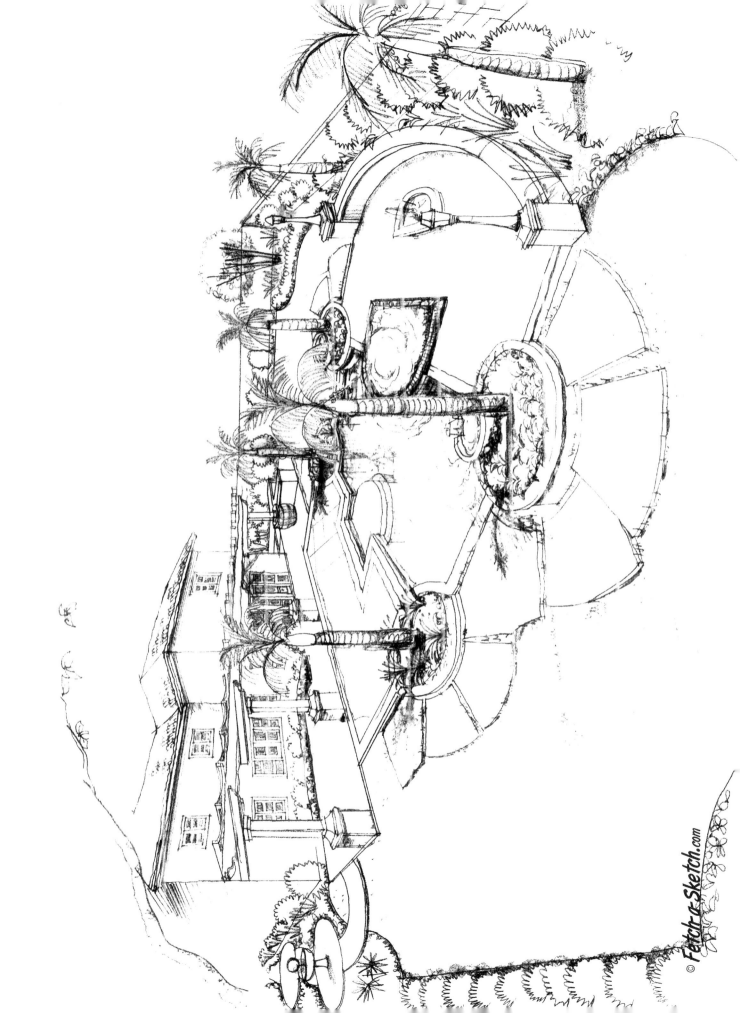

© Fetch-a-Sketch.com

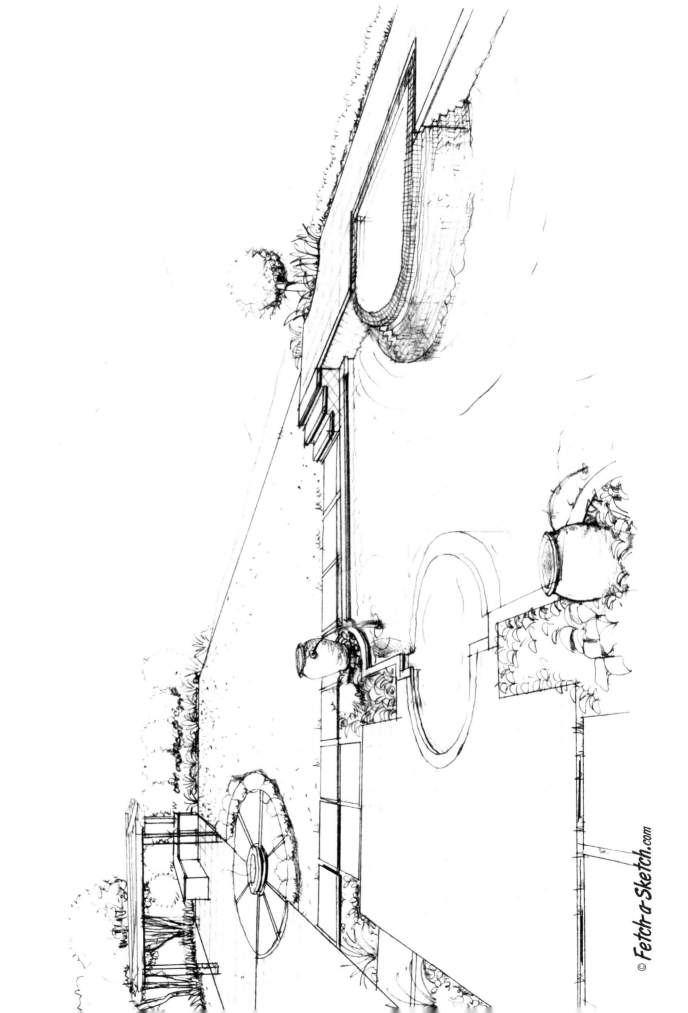

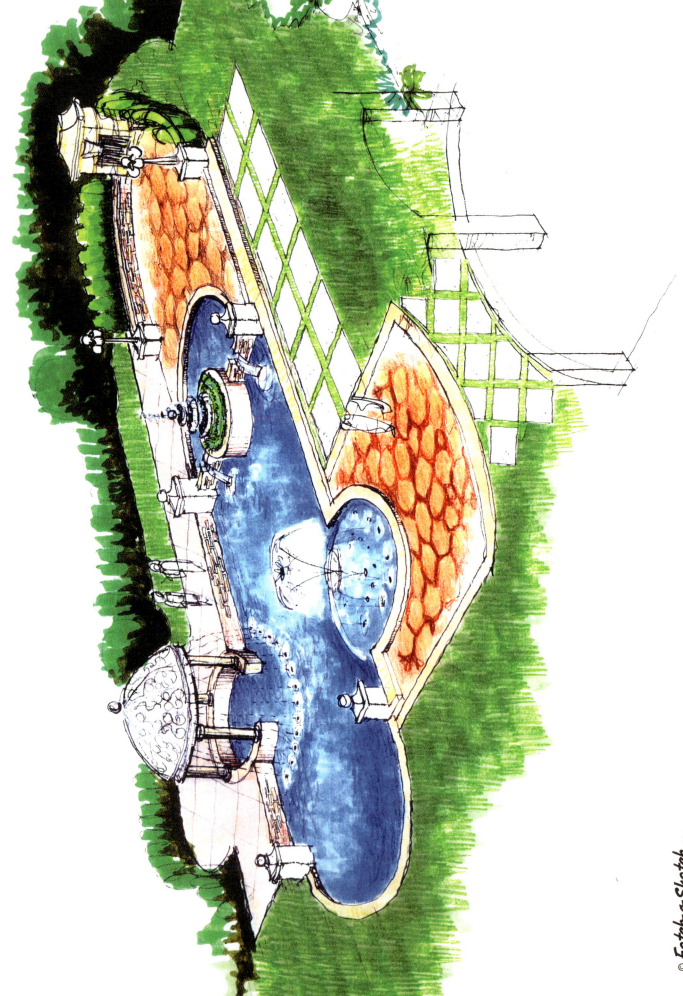

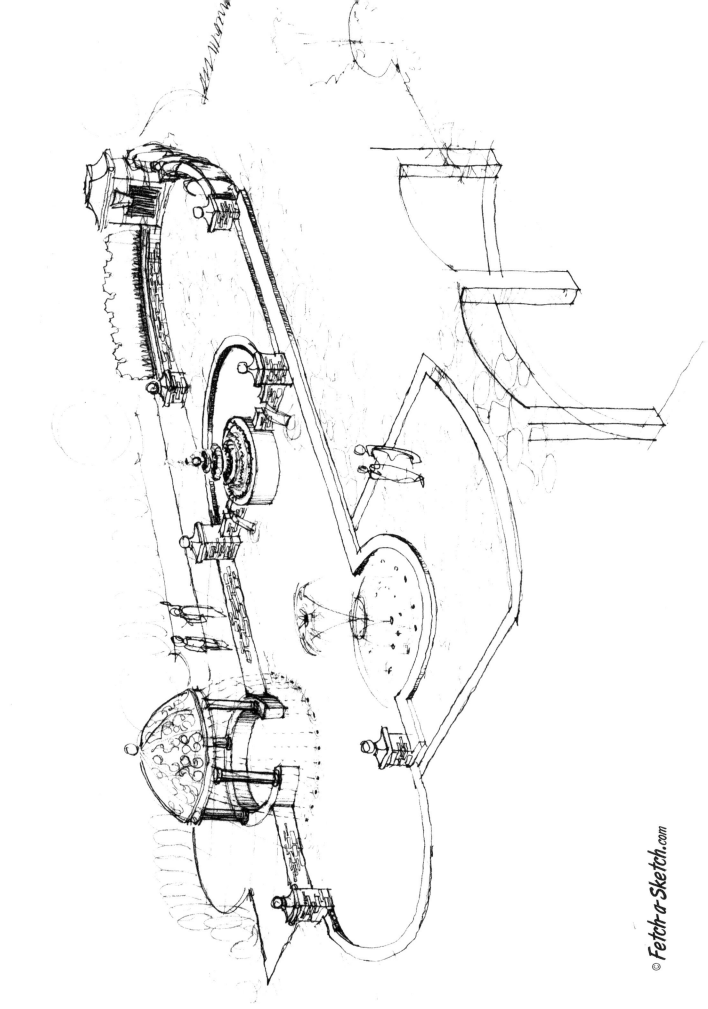

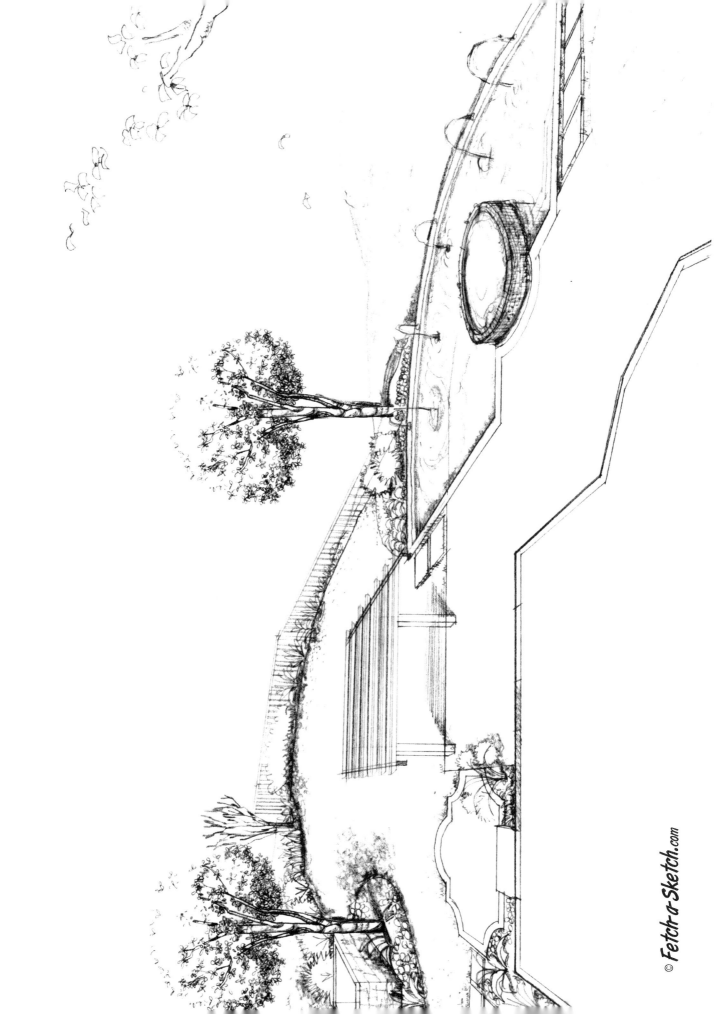

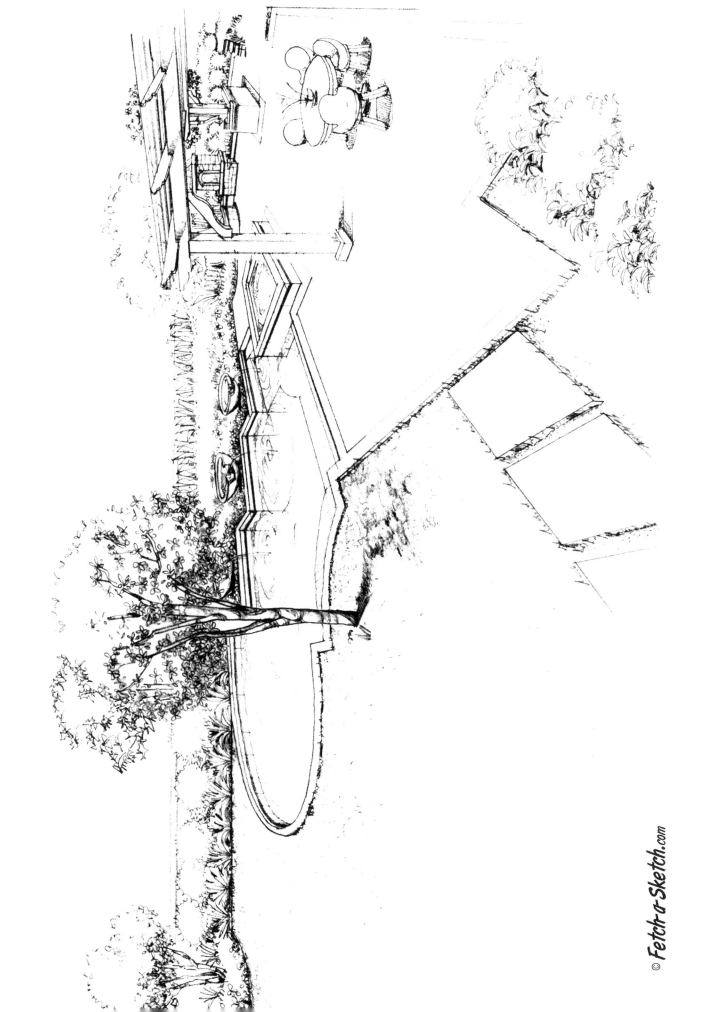

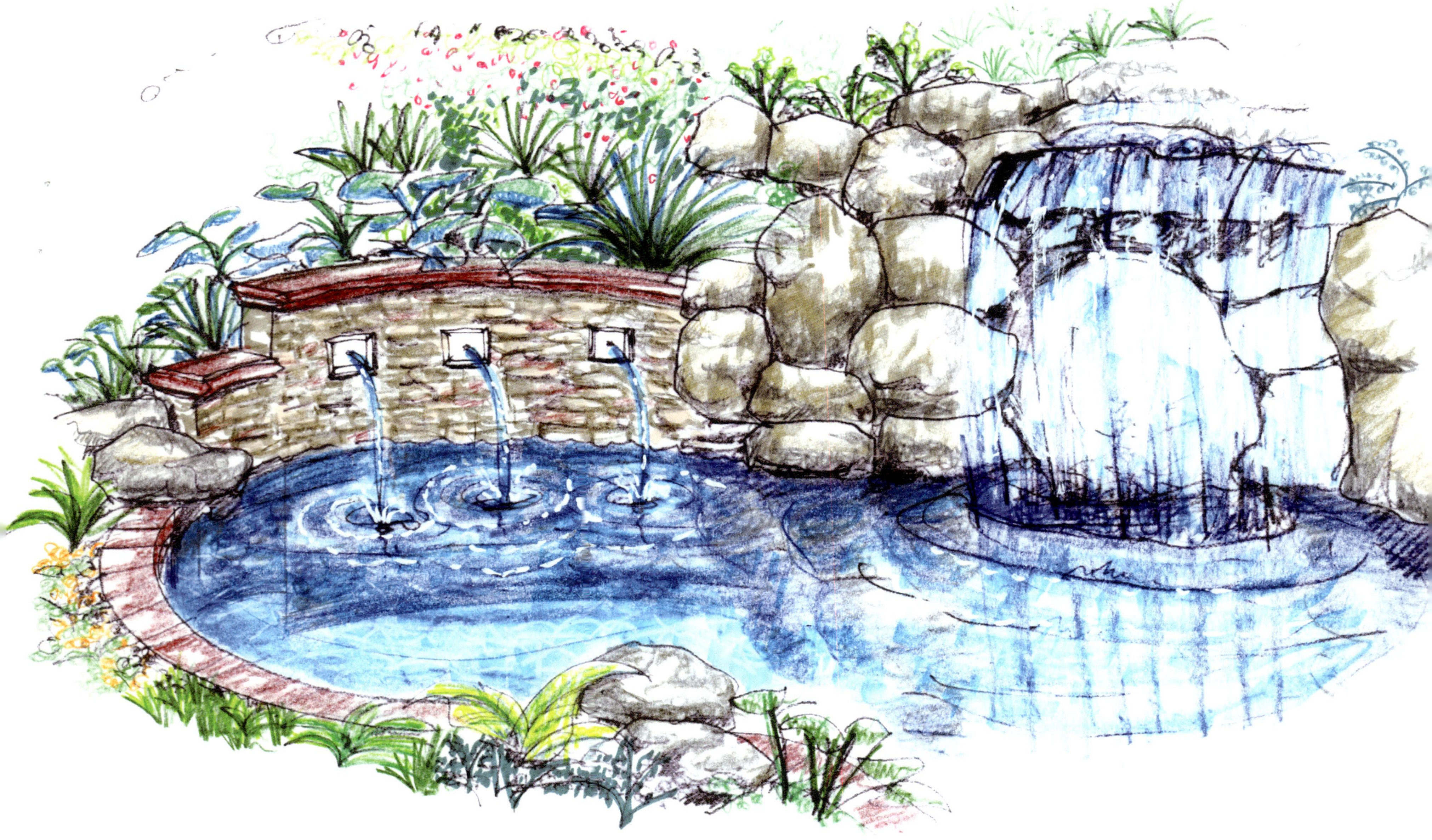

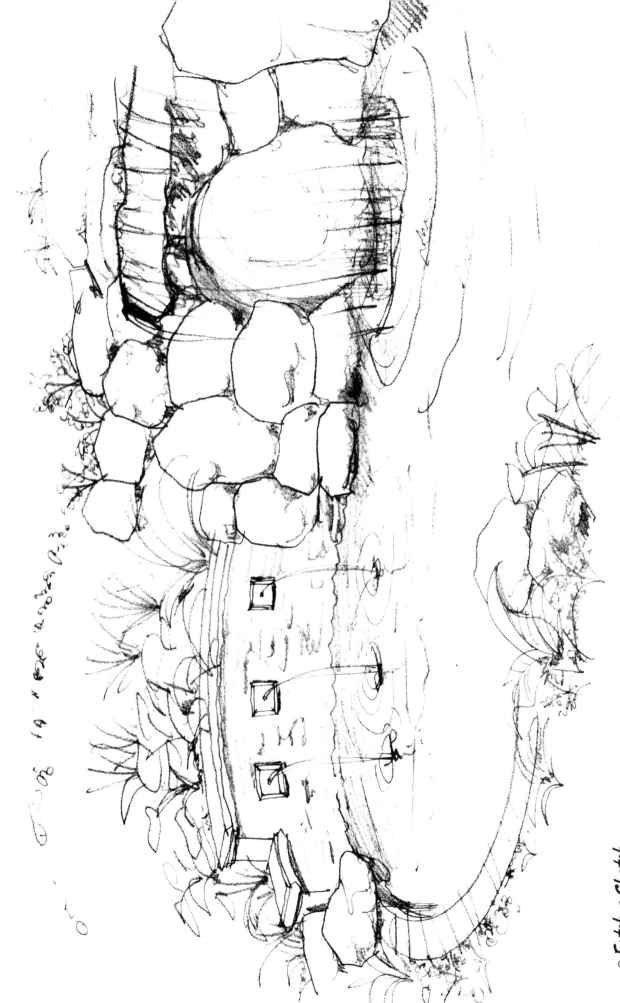

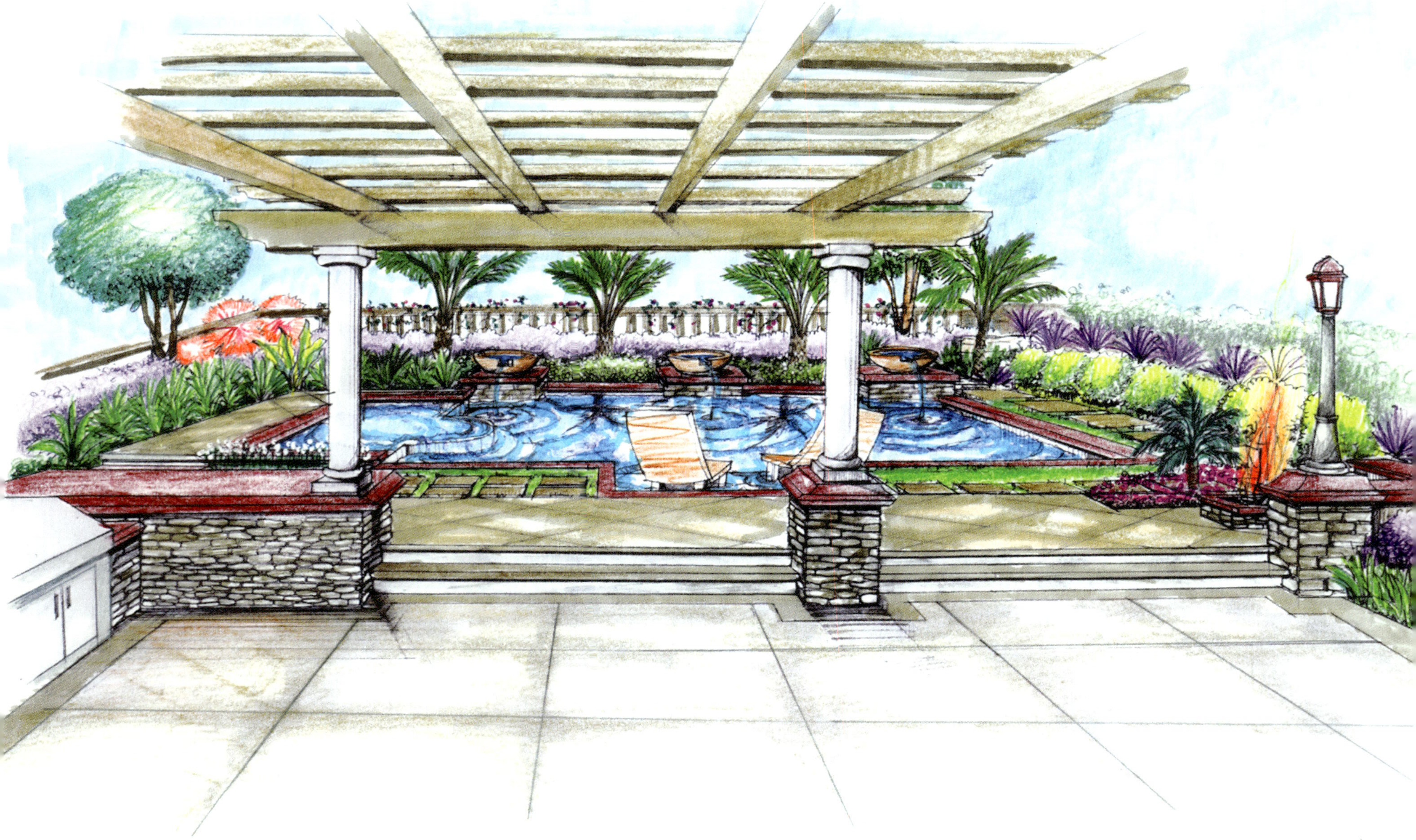

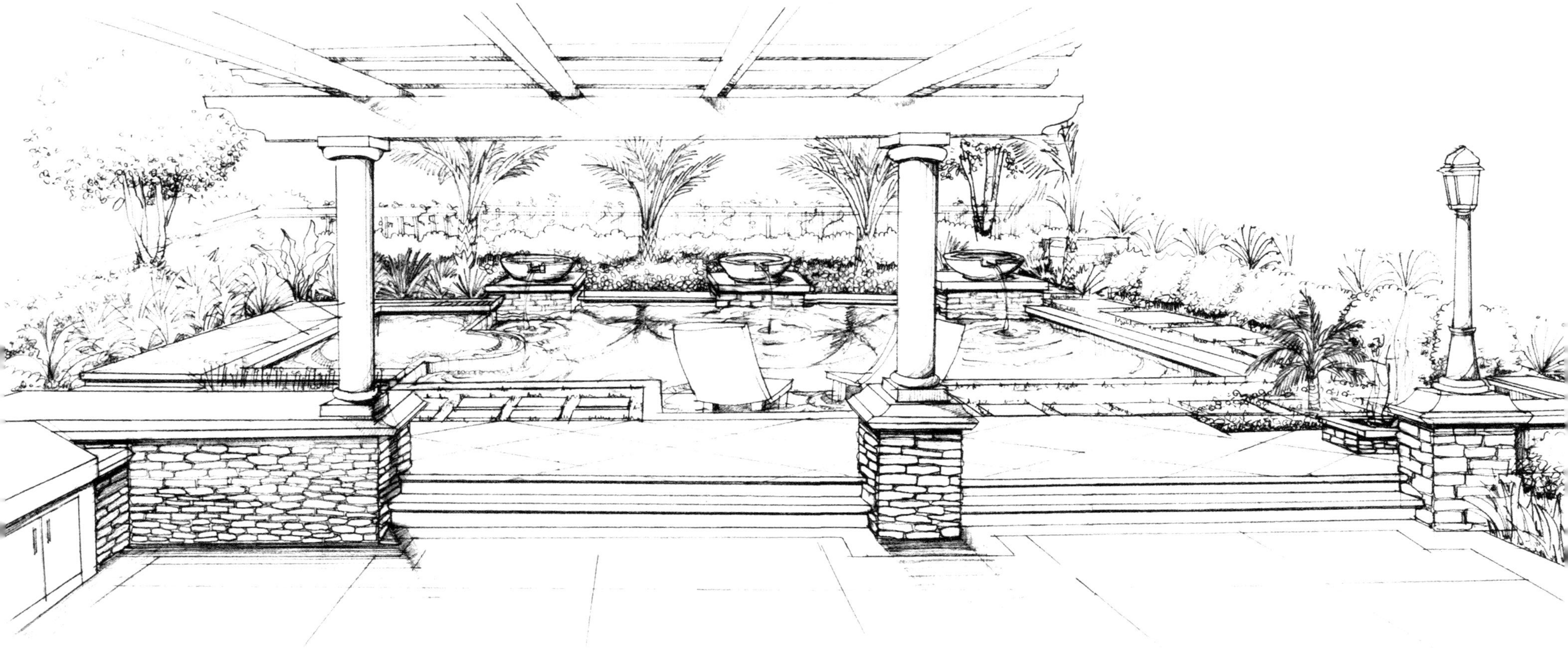

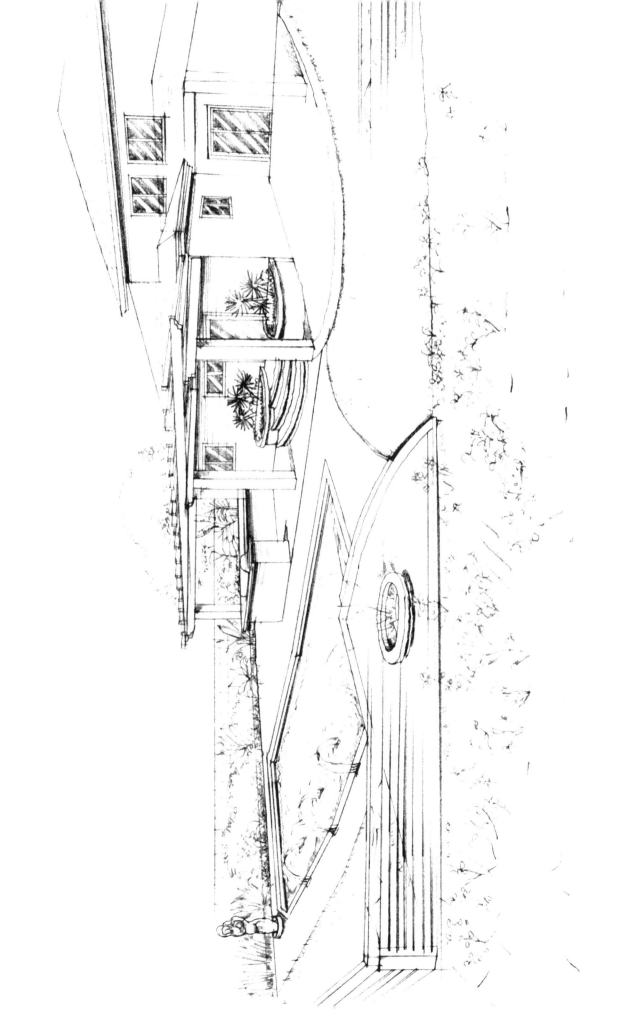

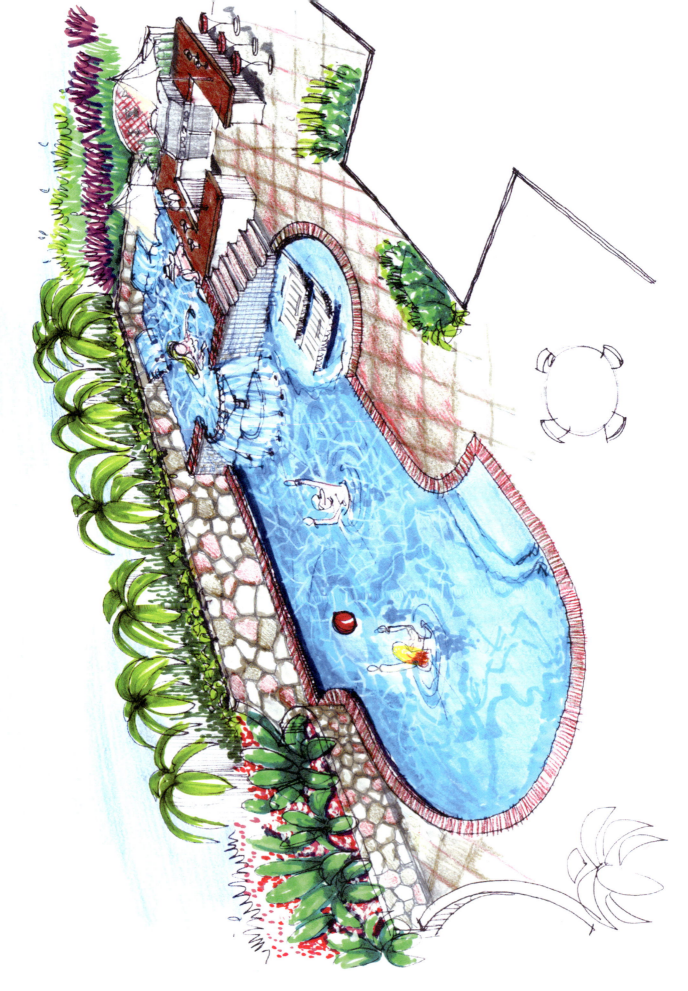

Buy Perspective Drawings at Fetch-A-Sketch.com

FETCH-A-SKETCH DRAWINGS USER AGREEMENT

The images in this book are owned by "Fetch-A-Sketch.com" an e-commerce web site and division of Intellectual Property Sales, Inc. The drawings are conceptual in nature and intended to be used as tools to inspire ideas and spruce up your sales presentations. They are not intended to be used as construction plans.

By purchasing this book, Pool and Spa Perspectives -((Volume 2) , You are buying a non-exclusive license to copy one or more individual Designer Content drawings and use the drawing for the following Permitted Uses:

(a)   You may make a copy and use that Licensed Concept Drawing as a starting point to create, or to commission a duly qualified and licensed design professional to create, the architectural and/or construction drawings necessary to construct the home improvement project depicted in the Licensed Concept Drawing.

(b)   If you are a design professional, you may include the print of the Licensed Concept Drawing among the design concepts that you present to the public in connection with promoting your professional services, but only subject to the prohibitions against removing copyright notice and making false claims of authorship as provided below.

(c)   In connection with either of the Permitted Uses described above, you may modify, edit, expand upon or otherwise alter the print copy of the Licensed Concept Drawing so as to create a Derivative Work under copyright law, and thereafter make one print of that Derivative Work and use that print for any Permitted Use. All Derivative Works shall be included within the term Licensed Concept Drawing as used elsewhere in this Agreement.

Prohibited Uses

Any use of a Licensed Concept Drawing that is not a Permitted Use as defined above violates this Agreement and constitutes copyright infringement. In particular, but without limitation, you may not:

(a)   re-sell, sub-license, distribute, publish or display Licensed Concept Drawings, except as specifically allowed by one of the Permitted Uses. For example, a design professional may show a Licensed Concept Drawing to a customer to illustrate the type of home improvement project that design professional might undertake, but may not sell a copy of that Licensed Concept Drawing or charge a fee for showing the Licensed Concept Drawing to the customer;

(b)   use any Licensed Concept Drawing as part of a trademark, service mark, logo, or in promotional advertising;

(c)   remove, alter or obscure any copyright notice, trademark or other legal rights designation from any place where it is embedded in the Licensed Concept Drawing;

(d)   use the Licensed Concept Drawing in design template applications intended for resale, whether online or not, including, without limitation, web site templates and brochure design templates;

(e)   use or display any Licensed Concept Drawing on a web site, through any telecommunications network or by wireless transmission or

by any other means now or hereafter created other than by physical delivery of the print on which the Licensed Concept Drawing resides;

(f)   falsely represent that you are the author of a Licensed Concept Drawing, but you may truthfully represent that you are the author of any new, original elements added by you to a Licensed Concept Drawing to create a Derivative Work.

Designer Content appearing in this book are presented solely for the purpose of illustrating concepts for home improvement projects. The Designer Content is not to scale, does not constitute and may not be used or relied upon as working drawings, construction drawings or any other form of drawings or plans suitable or capable of being constructed or built. If you desire to construct or install any home improvement project illustrated by any Designer Content drawing, it is your responsibility to have a qualified architect, contractor or other design professional prepare all required plans and drawings and secure all permits and permissions required by all laws, regulations and ordinances applicable to the project in question.

Intellectual Property Sales, Inc. does not make any warranty, representation or undertaking regarding the quality, characteristics, suitability, buildability or other attribute of the Designer Content.

Resources:

The Green Scene
6810 Canoga Ave., Canoga Park, CA. 91303
(818) 227-0740
GreenSceneLandscape.com

Fetch-A-Sketch.com
PoolDesignIdeas.com
ScottCohenDesigns.com

About the Author

Scott Cohen in his creative workspace

Scott Cohen is a nationally acclaimed garden artisan whose award winning work is frequently featured on Home and Garden Television and in numerous national books and magazines. He's known for his unique use of recycled materials, expert detailing, and innovative ceramic techniques to create stunning and functional outdoor environments.

Cohen is president and supervising designer of The Green Scene, a premier outdoor design and construction firm based in Los Angeles, California. He provides consultation for clients nationwide and gives seminars on designing outdoor kitchens and rooms, cast concrete techniques, and other topics for swimming pool and landscape professionals.

Buy 2 or more and save!

$ 29.95 for the 1st book and $ 20.00 each additional

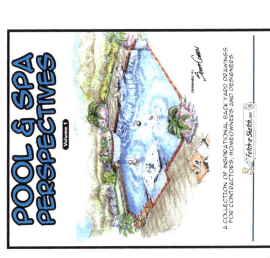

POOL & SPA PERSPECTIVES
Volume 1

A COLLECTION OF INSPIRATIONAL BACK YARD DRAWINGS FOR CONTRACTORS, HOMEOWNERS AND DESIGNERS

DESIGNED BY Ben Casas

Fetch-a-Sketch.com

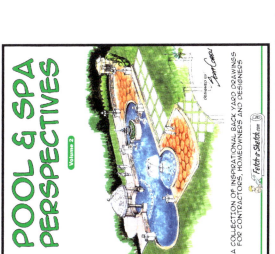

POOL & SPA PERSPECTIVES
Volume 2

A COLLECTION OF INSPIRATIONAL BACK YARD DRAWINGS FOR CONTRACTORS, HOMEOWNERS AND DESIGNERS

DESIGNED BY Ben Casas

Fetch-a-Sketch.com

POOL & SPA PERSPECTIVES
Volume 3

A COLLECTION OF INSPIRATIONAL BACK YARD DRAWINGS FOR CONTRACTORS, HOMEOWNERS AND DESIGNERS

DESIGNED BY Ben Casas

Fetch-a-Sketch.com

100 different design ideas

Due to popular demand we have created two more volumes!

Order Form

Name:

Billing Address:

City, State, Zip:

Shipping Address (if different)

City, State, Zip:

Billing Phone # ( )

Cell/Alternate Phone # ( )

E-mail Address

Card Type: Visa   Mastercard   AmEx   Discover

Card #

Exp: MM/YY _____ / _____   Signature _____

	Quantity	Book cost: 1 book $29.99, $20.00 each additional
☐ Volume 1		
☐ Volume 2		
☐ Volume 3		
Subtotal		
CA Sales Tax 9.25%		
Shipping		Shipping cost: 1 book $4.99, $1.99 each additional
Total		

Intellectual Property Sales Inc. 6810 Canoga Ave. Canoga Park. CA. 91303   (800) 813-8422